Hackathons

Andreas Kohne • Volker Wehmeier

Hackathons

From Idea to
Successful Implementation

 Springer

Andreas Kohne
Materna TMT GmbH
Dortmund, Germany

Volker Wehmeier
Bechtle GmbH
Hannover, Germany

ISBN 978-3-030-58838-0   ISBN 978-3-030-58839-7   (eBook)
https://doi.org/10.1007/978-3-030-58839-7

Translated and Extended from the German language edition: Hackathons - Von der Idee zur erfolgreichen Umsetzung by Andreas Kohne, © Springer Fachmedien Wiesbaden GmbH, ein Teil von Springer Nature 2019. Published by Springer Fachmedien Wiesbaden. All Rights Reserved.

This Springer imprint is published by the registered company Springer Nature Switzerland AG.
The registered company address is: Gewerbestrasse 11, 6330 Cham, Switzerland

Preface

Over the last 10 years, hackathons have become a real phenomenon. They started their success story many years ago in the USA and have since taken the whole world by storm. Hackathons are called the new "LAN parties" or "disruptive brainstorming." Started as pure software development meetings, they can now be found in many different areas and industries. What used to take place in small groups and dark rooms can now be found in schools, universities as well as in companies and public authorities as professionally organized events. Where once only "nerds" could be found, today self-confident entrepreneurs, socially committed do-gooders, highly talented software developers, musicians, technology fans, and people who are simply looking for a new challenge gather.

At hackathons, new technology should first be tried out in the shortest possible time, existing systems should be optimized and extended, or errors should be removed from software. The first hackathons lasted between 24 and 48 h and often took place on weekends. Gradually, however, mainly young start-ups discovered these events and used them to discuss their (mostly technical) business models at an early stage and to create a functioning prototype within a very short time, which in turn should encourage venture capitalists to invest money in the companies. At the same time, HR departments discovered hackathons as a powerful tool with a double effect in times of shortage of skilled workers: on the one hand, HR managers could observe many new applicants at work in a very short time and invite the best ones directly to job interviews, and on the other hand, a hackathon can create a positive corporate image. In the meantime, there are hackathons on various topics and with different durations and results. In recent years, they have been raised to become ever larger events with media coverage and large-scale sponsoring. The events fit the zeitgeist of agile work and offer many advantages and possibilities for organizers and participants.

Running a successful hackathon is no trivial task. Hackathons require a very complex preparation, a well-structured execution, and a conscious follow-up. The planning, execution, and follow-up have many aspects which are described in detail in the course of this book. First of all, you have to think about what the real driver or reason behind a hackathon is and what the goal is. Only then can the theme be determined, participants and sponsors invited and a suitable location booked. Also, keep in mind that besides positive motives and chances, there are also risks which should be known to everyone in advance and which should be averted (as far as possible) in advance. Here, above all, the complex legal aspects should be mentioned, which above all regulate the intellectual property rights of the ideas developed. Hackathons cost time and money. It is therefore all the more important to understand these events holistically in order to be able to carry them out optimally within the framework of the goals set.

This book provides a comprehensive overview of the topic of hackathons. At first, the basics and the history of hackathons are described in Chap. 1. Afterwards, the three phases of a hackathon are described in detail. This is started in Chap. 2 with the description of the individual measures which are to be accomplished before the actual event. Here not only technical or organizational aspects are described, but also the important legal aspects are discussed. Subsequently, it is shown what is necessary to carry out a hackathon successfully. For this purpose, the actual execution with all its steps is described in Chap. 3. Next, Chap. 4 looks at the follow-up. Unfortunately, it is often neglected or even completely forgotten. Chapter 5 describes from a participant's point of view the reasons for participating in a hackathon and which aspects guarantee a successful participation. In Chap. 6, the criticism of the format of the hackathons and their execution is also examined in detail. Finally, the most important points are summarized in Chap. 7 and Chap. 8 gives a view into the future of hackathons. In Chap. 9, statements and opinions of representatives from industry, science, and administration on the topic hackathons are presented in the form of quotations. The book is rounded off in Chap. 10 with detailed checklists, which you can use for the successful planning, operation, and follow-up of your own hackathons.

Dortmund, Germany   Andreas Kohne
Hannover, Germany   Volker Wehmeier

Contents

Basics

1

Abstract

Hackathons have become an international phenomenon in recent years. They originated from the first meeting of computer-loving technicians in the USA and have since spread to all continents. There are different types and goals of hackathons. Hackathons are held to try out new technologies, to exchange ideas between like-minded people, to recruit and finance start-ups. Hackathons usually last between 12 and 48 h and often take place on weekends. In order to run your own hackathon, a lot of planning work has to be done in advance. Many small things have to be taken into account during the operation as well. Above all, a follow-up is usually neglected or even completely forgotten.

In this chapter you will learn more about the history, the goals, and the course of hackathons.

Hackathons have become more and more popular in recent years and are now held in all parts of the world on various topics. The word *hackathon* is composed of the two words "to hack" and "marathon" (the famous 42 km run). Hackathons can be found under many names by now: Hack Fest, Hack Days, Code Days, Code Fest, and many more. The procedure is more or less the same at all events: a group of people meet for a pre-defined period of time to work together in small groups on new ideas or technologies and produce something new in the shortest possible time. At the end of the event, the developed ideas and prototypes are then presented to the group and usually also to a jury. In the meantime, prize money or material prizes are often awarded to the winners.

What sounds so simple here can become very large and very complex on closer inspection. The number of participants can range from just under a dozen to several thousand people. The duration is usually limited to 24–48 h. But there are also outliers upwards. So there are hackathons that stretch over several months. But they break with some of the standards and are rather a marginal phenomenon.

One reason why hackathons have become so popular is the unpredictability of the results. This is why more and more people with different technical and social backgrounds participate and companies and investors especially support this format. In the worst case scenario, a few new ideas are tried out that do not have much use. At least the participants were able to exchange ideas with like-minded people and hopefully had fun at the event. In the best case, the foundation stone for a new multimillion-dollar company is laid. The chance to be part of such an event, to be able to invest money in the "next big thing," or to develop a groundbreaking product idea for one's own company is what makes these events so attractive.

Hackathons usually deal with very technical topics and often involve the development or enhancement of software in the broadest sense. There are also hackathons that deal with hardware or combinations of hardware and software. In recent years the idea of hackathons has been exported from the technical field to many other areas. There are now hackathons on topics such as music, (computer) games, health, environment, and culture. Young entrepreneurs often make targeted use of hackathons to discuss and develop their new business ideas, meet venture capitalists, and convince them of the idea. The character of hackathons has changed massively in recent years. They changed from weekend meetings of enthusiastic "nerds" to fully commercialized large-scale events with sponsors and a large media presence. In order to understand this change, the history of the hackathons is described in detail in the next section.

1.1   History

According to Jonathan Gottfried, co-founder of Major League Hacking, the roots of the hackathons lie already in the late 1970s in the USA (see [3] and [4]). There, computer-loving programmers and hardware tinkerers met regularly in the so-called Homebrew Computer Club. The computers of that time were by far not comparable with today's PCs. Instead, there were various platforms and systems. In those days, the computers mostly had to be assembled by hand and partly had to be run with self-developed hardware and software. During this time the first "nerds" met in small groups to improve their systems, correct errors, and exchange and implement ideas for further developments.

The actual term "hackathon" was first used in 1999 for a meeting of OpenBSD[1] developers, who met for a weekend in Calgary, Alberta, Canada to fix known bugs in the operating system and to add new network protocols to the system. A total of ten highly specialized developers were found, who worked exclusively on these topics for just under 3 days. Almost simultaneously and completely independent of the OpenBSD meeting, the company Sun Microsystems called for a developer

---

[1]OpenBSD is a Linux-based operating system which is provided as free open source software and is constantly developed by volunteers. Official homepage: https://www.openbsd.org/.

meeting, also under the name hackathon, to develop new software for the then very popular pocket communicator "Palm Pilot" (a predecessor of the current tablets).

After these two hackathons it became quiet around the topic again. This does not mean, however, that there were no meetings of developers on hardware or software topics in the following years. The meetings simply did not (yet) have much importance and were held exclusively locally or even privately. In 2005, an event was founded in San Francisco called "SuperHappyDevHouse." Interested hackers met over a weekend in a private house, developed new projects, or improved existing systems. There was a bit of partying and in the end the results were presented in the group. These events still exist today.

It was not until 2006 that the topic came back to a wider public. The then very successful internet company Yahoo organized the first large-scale hackathon named the "Hack Day". The big difference between previous events was that this was the first time that it was an open competition. The aim was to bring together internal developers and external interested parties to develop new ideas together in a short time. This can be seen as the birth of modern hackathons with prizes and sponsors.

Just 1 year later, the first hackathon named "Startup Week" was held in 2007 which had the goal of creating the basis for a new company in the shortest possible time. Here, 70 participants were already working on a solution which, with the help of new software, would enable rapid coordination between large groups of people. This event can be seen as the starting point for the commercialization of the hackathons. From this point on, the goal was to quickly develop new and profitable business models and to create a first working prototype. "Startup Week" events have been taking place regularly ever since all over the world.

The next thing that changed was not so much the actual course or goal of the hackathons, but rather the topics and the participants. In 2009 the first "Music Hack Day" was held in New York. The goal was to develop interesting new solutions by combing musicians and developers. Several hundred people came to this event. What is interesting about this format is that it is directly based on Yahoo's "Hack Day" and the entire organization and the process was made available as an open source document so that anyone interested can develop and host their own hackathon on this basis.

In 2010 the first hackathon for students was held by "hackNY." More than 100 students came together for a weekend with the goal of developing crazy new technical ideas. The event was a complete success and can be seen as the starting signal for the now worldwide widespread student hackathons. No serious problems are to be solved or new business models developed. The goal is simply to create something new with fun using new technology and get into a very intensive and direct exchange with other students. For example, one of the winners has developed a respiratory measuring device that prohibits the upload of new program code into the cloud-based software management system "GIT" above a certain alcohol level.

In 2010, a hackathon was held for the first time in New York by "TechCrunch Disrupt," which had almost 600 participants. The goal behind the first event was to bring hackathons to New York on a grand scale, to encourage collaboration among developers, and to try out new technologies. The event was a huge success and has been repeated many times. One of the projects of the first event was called "groop.ly." This involved developing the prototype of a software that allowed a group of people to conduct group chats over the internet. The project did not win the hackathon at that time. But the developers believed in their idea and started to develop the software further. Shortly after the hackathon they founded a start-up and called themselves "GroupMe." The young company then received 10.6 million dollars from venture capitalists to ensure rapid growth. Just 1 year later, the company was bought by Skype (which in turn had been bought by Microsoft) for almost 80 million dollars. This success of a company that had been founded during a hackathon changed everything. From then on, the focus of the big hackathons was almost exclusively on start-ups. The investors and young entrepreneurs fell into a kind of gold-digger mood and the hackathons became bigger and bigger and supported by bigger and bigger sponsors.

One year later, in 2011, the University of Pennsylvania in Philadelphia held the first "PennApps" hackathon. Unlike previous hackathons, this one was the first to open nationwide and attracted hundreds of students from all over the USA. From this point on the rapid spread of the hackathons began. In 2013, "Mega Hacks" was the first time a hackathon was held with over 1000 participants. This event format quickly found a worldwide distribution and the hackathons became bigger and more international. The biggest hackathon so far was the "NASA Space Challenge" with more than 8000 participants from 44 countries. One of the most famous developments from a hackathon is certainly the dating app "Tinder" for smartphones. The idea for the app, which was initially called Matchbox, had already been developed by Sean Rad and Justin Mateen before the hackathon. During the event they built a first prototype. Shortly afterwards, it became a small company that was very successful in procuring risk capital. In the meantime, "Tinder" is the most used dating app worldwide with millions of users.

The hackathons described so far were all public hackathons. This means that basically everybody could participate in them. However, there is still a possibility to run hackathons in-house. Here the same rules apply, only that only employees of the respective company may participate. Many companies are already using the format of hackathons to develop new ideas and to create executable prototypes in a very short time. Many large companies regularly hold hackathons to generate fresh ideas that can improve their business. One of the best known results of an internal hackathon is the "like-button" of Facebook. The idea and the first implementation were born in the context of an internal Facebook hackathon. Meanwhile the button is an integral part of the social media platform and is used on many other sites.

All in all, hackathons fit into the current zeitgeist, in which new ideas are developed quickly with the help of "Design Thinking" (see [8]), the so-called makers deal with the further development of technical and non-technical items (see [5]) and companies are increasingly managed in an agile way (see [1]). As can already be seen in this chapter, hackathons can pursue different goals. In the following section the possible goals of a hackathon will be presented in more detail.

1.2   Goals

The goal of the first hackathon was to "tinker" with technology and somehow make it smarter, faster, or better. Nowadays, hackathons are held in various places for various reasons. The most common goals of current hackathons are described below. First the goals of the big and openly advertised events are described.

1. ***Try out ideas/technologies:*** This is the original alignment of the hackathons. It is about testing the limits of new technology, combining different technologies in new ways, or complementing them to create something new. It is important to note that most of the time there are no commercial intentions, and the participants who create these "hacks" have a passion for tinkering and programming. Such hackathons are often found in university environments, are often carried out relatively locally, and often do not have extremely high numbers of participants.

    Sometimes large technology companies also provide new hardware or software within the framework of hackathons, in order to let people find out within a short time what this technology can be used for. These hackathons certainly have a focus on future products and they usually reward the winners with highly endowed cash or material prizes. Such events are often widely advertised, attract many participants, and are often international in scope.

2. ***Promoting start-ups:*** Another goal of the open hackathons is to give start-ups the opportunity to present their ideas to a larger audience at a very early stage, to develop first prototypes, and to arrange contacts to developers. The main reason, however, is to present new ideas to venture capitalists and, if possible, to find investors for a new company. Such hackathons often find people with new and sometimes very stubborn and creative business ideas and technically very skilled developers looking for a new job. Often new companies are founded after a hackathon, which continue working on the basis of the idea developed during the event or the already implemented prototype and whose employees were participants of the hackathon. These hackathons are usually very well attended and serve as a job, business idea, and financing hub, where often large donors invest a lot of venture capital and hope to find the "next big thing."

After the goals of external hackathons have been examined, the most common goals of internal hackathons are described below.

1. ***Driving innovation:*** In recent years companies have often relied on hackathons to quickly develop new business or product ideas. For this purpose, employees from different areas are brought together on a special topic, a technology, or without further specifications in order to develop new ideas in the shortest possible time (for example, over a weekend), which can then be further examined in a next step. Sometimes these hackathons are also intentionally opened to external parties in order to bring in further ideas from outside and to have people around who can bring "fresh wind."

It should be noted that such hackathons are no substitute for an internal product development or research unit. Innovation cannot be forced and cannot be "outsourced" to events. These events exclusively offer the possibility to quickly develop new ideas or to promptly transfer ideas from product development into a prototype. The transfer into marketable products and the testing of the products on the market can of course not be done by hackathons. Rather, they should be seen as an additional source of innovation, offering fun and creative enjoyment for your employees with a new format.

2. **Recruiting:** The next goal of hackathons in companies is to gain new personnel. Hackathons are offered here, which are either enriched with internal developers or exclusively filled with external applicants. The goal is to get an impression of the applicants within a short time. Hackathons offer an excellent opportunity for this, as all participants have to be very creative under high time pressure. Furthermore, an impression of the technical expertise of the developers can be gained quickly. In addition, the participants of the individual groups have to exchange a lot of information under stress and there is a lot of communication within the groups, between the groups, and with the organizer. Here, impressions of the participants' social skills (see [11]) can be gained quickly. These hackathons are often carried out by employees from the human resources department together with specialist contact persons from the respective departments. Usually the prizes are not only cash or material prizes, but also internships or employment. Sometimes these hackathons are therefore called "Assessment Center 2.0."

3. **Teambuilding:** Internal hackathons can also be used to improve the morale of existing teams. The fresh format and the very intense collaboration under heavy time pressure can be very motivating for the team members and can weld them closer together. In these hackathons, just like recruitment-oriented hackathons, the focus is not necessarily on the actual result. Rather, it is about the event itself and the (hopefully positive) effects on the team. It is all the more pleasing, of course, when a valid business idea or product improvement is created at the same time.

4. **Increase external perception:** Another goal of corporate hackathons is to position themselves externally as an innovative, active, and flexible company. This should enhance the company's image and attract more applicants in times of skill shortages (especially in IT). This is often included as a side effect of recruiting hackathons. Hackathons are very topical right now and can be applied very well via social media (such as Facebook, Twitter, and LinkedIn). This means that even smaller companies can quickly achieve a certain media reach.

1.3   Procedure

Running your own hackathon requires a lot of planning and a precise idea of what should happen when. Basically, a hackathon can be divided into three phases. The phases of a hackathon are shown graphically in Fig. 1.1.

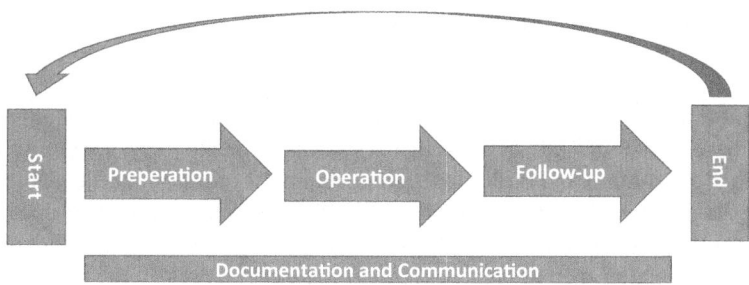

Fig. 1.1 General procedure of a hackathon

1. ***Preparation:*** This first phase is by far the longest and is often underestimated in its complexity. This is where a detailed plan of the actual hackathon is drawn up to ensure that the execution goes smoothly afterwards. It should start with basic things like the goal and theme of the hackathon. Then a date, a suitable location, personnel, and much more is needed. Also the legal framework and the conditions of participation have to be planned carefully so that there will be no problems later on. In addition, a jury, sponsors, and possibly media partners are needed for reporting. In Chap. 2 all aspects of successful planning are presented in detail. Other good sources for planning your own hackathon are "https://hackathon.guide" und "https://hackdaymanifesto.com."

2. ***Operation:*** The second phase is the actual operation. Hackathons usually follow a very similar procedure. At the beginning the participants are received. Afterwards a short introductory lecture is often given to motivate the basic topic and to explain the technical and organizational framework. Afterwards, individual persons introduce themselves with their ideas, which they want to tackle in the course of the hackathon. Then the participants get together in the groups that are most interesting for them and the work begins. Depending on the planned length of the hackathon, work will then begin on the content. In the end the results are presented in the plenum and in front of the jury. The hackathon is concluded with an award ceremony.

   To make the hackathon as smooth as possible, good planning is also necessary. A detailed description of all necessary steps can be found in Chap. 3.

3. ***Follow-up:*** The third and last phase is often neglected or even completely forgotten or intentionally omitted. However, this is precisely where considerable added value can arise. This is where the results can be followed up professionally, connections to investors and sponsors can be established, and new companies can possibly be founded. This requires a lot of know-how, which can be conveyed to interested participants in the course of a professional follow-up. In the case of internal hackathons, which had the goal of producing a product or business model innovation, the ideas developed must be extensively examined and tested for their marketability in the follow-up to the hackathon. Should a valid business idea emerge, it must be transferred to the actual product development in a previously

defined process and further advanced. In Chap. 4 the steps for a successful follow-up are described in detail.

All three phases should be accompanied by continuous communication. This means that you should advertise your hackathon from the very beginning of the planning. Report often and through different channels (online and offline) how your planning is progressing. During the hackathon you should report very intensively. Use one or more team members and possibly the press for this. You should continue to communicate after the hackathon. Report on the event, present the results and the winners. Maybe you can already announce the next hackathon.

In addition to the accompanying communication, you should write down everything you do during each phase, plan, and decide. Document everything. From the first idea, plans, requests, offers, negotiation processes, and results, positive and negative. Also record who did what when and who has to do what by when. In this way you ensure that every step can be traced. Furthermore, your documentation can be used afterwards to evaluate the hackathon and the whole process and to learn for the next event. This way you make sure that you get better from time to time.

1.4   Summary

- The word hackathon is composed of the words "to hack" and "marathon."
- Hackathons are events where creative new ideas are developed and tested with a group of people in a very short time (usually between 24 and 48 h). These ideas are then presented in plenary sessions and in front of a jury. The best results are often awarded with cash or material prizes.
- Hackathons come from the USA and were initially meetings of technology-enthusiastic "nerds" who wanted to try out new technologies and supplement or improve existing systems (hardware or software).
- In the meantime, hackathons are often very commercial. Many venture capitalists look for good investment opportunities and sponsors promote their companies and products. Often the events are strongly accompanied by media (online and offline).
- In recent years, hackathons have been held all over the world and often hundreds or even thousands of people take part.
- Hackathons are often technology-driven. But there are also hackathons on many other topics, such as music, (computer) games, health, environment, and culture.
- Hackathons can be advertised as an open event in which anyone interested can take part, or they can be held internally within a company.
- The main goals of modern hackathons are: Trying out new ideas and technologies, promoting start-ups, driving innovation, recruiting, team building, and enhancing the corporate image.
- Good online sources for planning a hackathon: "https://hackdaymanifesto.com" and "https://hackdaymanifesto.com."

- Running a successful hackathon requires three phases: Preparation (see Chap. 2), operation (see Chap. 3), and follow-up (see Chap. 4). Each of these phases should be planned in detail and run through with the utmost care to ensure a smooth process.
- Communicate a lot and during each phase. Use online and offline communication.
- Document every step and every decision. This will help you evaluate the hackathon afterwards, learn from your mistakes, and get better each time.

Preparation

2

Abstract

To organize a successful hackathon many things have to be considered, planned, and prepared in advance. This chapter gives an overview of the most important points you should consider when planning. This ranges from simple things like date, duration, topic, and number of participants to the right location, your team, technology, sponsors, costs, and legal aspects that should be considered already during the planning.

Running a hackathon event means unwinding a previously prepared implementation plan. Accordingly, improvisation is only possible during the implementation in case of deviations from the plan. During the preparation of a hackathon there is enough time to prepare for all eventualities and to think through the challenges of the successful event. Therefore, this chapter will address as comprehensively as possible the points that need to be considered in advance. Every organizer will want to make his event a special one and will therefore evaluate the points individually for himself. The preparation phase involves a lot of brainstorming. Here you should start early to record thoughts and let them flow into the preparatory written planning.

The individual activities of the preparation are shown graphically in Fig. 2.1.

© The Author(s), under exclusive license to Springer Nature Switzerland AG 2020
A. Kohne, V. Wehmeier, *Hackathons*,
https://doi.org/10.1007/978-3-030-58839-7_2

2.1 Organizer and Participants

While the private sector can maintain its sustainability through innovation, the public sector will be able to enhance its reputation with citizens and its image as a modern employer through fresh ideas. Universities see their core task in finding what has not been thought of so far, and even associations, parties, and lobbies benefit by channeling the energy, will, and power of many people's thoughts into new and creative paths. Good ideas are the currency of this century and are therefore valuable for everyone. Whether a hackathon offers the right answer to this insight will have to be decided individually. The number of participants in a hackathon can be very colorful, but there are also many possibilities as an organizer. In the following the most common groupings are presented in detail.

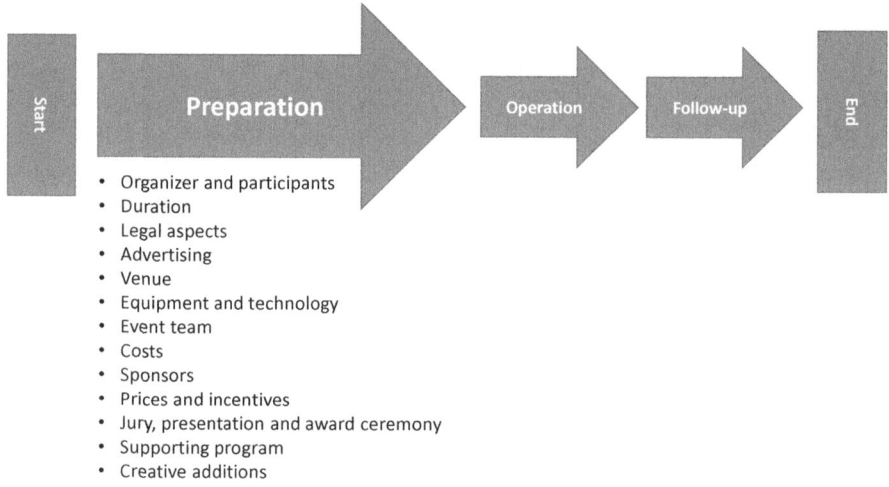

Fig. 2.1 Overview of the individual activities during the preparation

2.1.1 Corporate Hackathon

In almost every sector, the survival of companies depends on whether products and services can be offered on a permanent basis that reflect the state of technology and the spirit of the times. Above all, it is important to hold one's own in competition with other companies. Good marketing is not able to conceal an inadequate offer for long. A lot of energy can be generated from a format that is able to generate new impulses from different minds, lines of vision, knowledge disciplines, age groups, and social classes. Such impulses can be specifically triggered by a hackathon and can be aimed at various purposes. Here are some examples:

- Existing products or services are to be further developed.
- New product lines can be conceived and alternatives compared.

- Selected key technologies are jointly examined for their usability.
- Company suggestion scheme is set up as an annual event instead of a continuous process.
- Concrete problems of a company are put up for discussion and solutions are actively sought.
- The reorientation of the company is discussed jointly and creatively.

2.1.2 External Hackathon of a Corporation

The goals that a company can pursue with an internal hackathon can also be achieved by involving external participants. A motivation for this can result from being perceived as a modern employer. The recruitment of new employees from a hackathon is in practice often a desired goal. External participants are also valuable for the organizer because they are not subject to any "operational blindness" and bring with them other competency profiles. This often brings a fresh breeze and new ideas that would otherwise not be considered by internal employees. An external hackathon is much more complex to prepare and execute and more costly in terms of legal and marketing aspects. The rules must be defined very precisely and the event must be promoted externally at an early stage so that appropriate participants can be found. The objective compared to an internal hackathon is broader in the areas of external perception and employee recruitment. Therefore you should try to do everything to put your company in a good light during the hackathon. Purely internal hackathons can also be held in your own office. However, these are usually not representative enough to be used by external parties. Also the number of participants can be a limiting factor. So look for a suitable location early on.

2.1.3 A Government Agency Organizes a Hackathon

The civil service is often associated with cumbersomeness, backwardness, and slow pace. The fact that this is not true, but that there is a clear will to modernize and change, can also be documented publicly. Especially the assessment that a hackathon is not the typical format for further development should encourage decision-makers at federal, state, or local level to use this format. It can work with citizens and employees alike. Fields of application can be similar to the following:

- Criticism of tasks within the authority takes place with the employees.
- Proven but unpopular processes are examined for optimization potential.
- A long-standing municipal problem is examined with citizens for creative solution variants.
- A municipal planning process is enriched with experts and/or citizens by creative solution approaches.
- A technical solution is being sought for an official problem in the field of digitization.

2.1.4   Hackathon as Campus Event of a University

Universities follow a teaching and research mission, and both professors and students strive to be up-to-date and to generate the best academic careers and corresponding successes. It is not for nothing that the genesis of an overwhelming number of successful start-ups worldwide begins on a university campus. But even universities cannot generate ideas at the push of a button in the normal teaching process of the faculties. Away from the curriculum, it is easier to think through daily topics, technologies, and problem areas. This free space can result from the special nature of an event format like a hackathon. Fields of application can be here:

- A new technology is being tested in a competition on campus.
- An interesting topic is being promoted among the faculties of the university for a competitive test of strength.
- A question of the university itself is discussed with the involvement of the students.
- A company organizes a hackathon together with a university in order to be able to use third-party funds in a more targeted manner.

2.1.5   A Club Holding a Hackathon

Associations have a common interest in cultivating their purpose and the inherent theme, but also in developing it further. A beekeeper's association can be just as interested in progress as a club for the promotion of the local comprehensive school and also sports clubs can think about hackathons. Possible ideas could be the following:

- A mini-hackathon to acquire new members is started.
- A hackathon is held to get members more involved in a current issue.
- A club tries to connect its members with each other through a hackathon.
- A sub-discipline within the purpose of the association is to be further thought and developed.
- Creative new ways to bring money into the club treasury are being sought.
- New services are being developed for members or externals.

2.1.6   The Composition of Participants

One of the most important questions to be resolved is that of the composition of the participants. Who can and should participate at all? To what extent skills, life experience, and educational status may mix is up to the organizers. In most cases it will be difficult to define an exact description of the participants. An event is fresher when creative, motivated, and idealistic participants are on board. An event is more successful in its results if experienced and proven people allow you to share your experiences. Mixed teams and an interdisciplinary composition promise the best results.

So when planning your hackathon, pay close attention to who you are addressing as potential participants and match your requirements for a possible outcome with the invited participants. Think about the dimensions age, education, studies, seniority, and of course the personal motivation of the participants. Being together with people who are different from yourself makes people more creative, harder working, and more diligent.

By the way, you should also consider whether interested spectators are allowed to participate in your hackathon. This can also enrich the hackathon. In the run-up to the hackathon you should also consider whether you want to allow real professionals and professionals with experience in the hackathon. This can be positive for the quality of the results, but must not disadvantage students, young professionals, and less experienced competitors. Here it is important to create a balance through a clever mixture of different profiles in the later teams. In the end, the judges' sense of proportion is also required when evaluating the individual results.

2.1.7 All Age Groups

The format for hackathons is not yet finished and therefore the field of application is not limited. You can start a hackathon at the breakfast table with your children, and within 10 min you can bring up all kinds of ideas on a topic. And a hackathon in a retirement home can be just as electrifying if the topic and the participants are sufficiently well chosen. If the format of hackathons can only be associated with young, creative people, it would not be thought through to the end. In their own lives, young and old people think differently about solutions to their problems. The ability to evaluate problems is linked to experiential knowledge, just as creativity will never be reserved for young individuals. And even young people can always be an enrichment due to a wealth of ideas characterized by an unreserved way of thinking.

If possible, involve all age groups in your hackathon. At least try to keep the age range as large as possible. This way you will benefit from all the advantages and at the same time ensure a generation-spanning exchange.

2.1.8 The Right Size for a Hackathon

A hackathon that is too small does not create an atmosphere of power struggle. Since the effort required for a good hackathon is considerable, one should even think about a cancelation or postponement if the minimum number of participants is less than two dozen. Conversely, one should also consider a maximum number of participants in advance. A three-digit number of participants can already cause difficulties, because the evaluation of the results, the awarding of prizes, and the award ceremony become more complicated and time-consuming with a large number of participants. Hackathons that are too big often lose their atmosphere. Also, if the hackathons are too big, the participant may doubt whether he has a realistic chance of winning. Last but not least, the size of the hackathon must be adapted to the premises, the available budget, and the available coaches.

There is no concrete recommendation for an optimal number of participants. Try rather to estimate how many teams and thus how many new ideas you want to have generated and how large the teams should be on average. You can make a fairly good estimate of this.

After you have determined how many participants you want to include, you can control exactly how many participants will come to your hackathon via your invitation management and limited participant lists with move-up procedures.

2.1.9   The Composition of the Teams

Good results in hackathons are often achieved in teams made up of different disciplines and people with different backgrounds. Teams that are too large carry the risk that not all participants are equally involved and that only parts of the team will carry the creative output. Sometimes, however, outstanding achievements are also individual performances. In principle, it should therefore also be permissible to participate in the hackathon as an individual. But this is definitely a rarity.

Already in the run-up to a hackathon, potential participants need to know whether the organizer is counting on teams that already exist and perhaps have proven themselves, or whether individuals may only form teams shortly before the hackathon. Both make sense—the existing team can quickly get into the hackathon project, a new mixed team will possibly show more creativity. If the organizer plans to determine the team composition himself, this should be clearly stated in advance.

If the teams are only supposed to get together during the event, you have to allow for an appropriate time for this process at the beginning of the hackathon. Do not set too much time for this process, because fast and emotional decisions should be made here.

2.2   Duration

Time is a relative quantity and so the question arises about the correct duration of a hackathon execution. The length of a hackathon is also related to the seriousness, professionalism, and budget of the event. If more time is invested, higher quality results can be expected in the end. However, this thesis is only true if the task is varied and demanding enough. If there is no real challenge inherent in the hackathon, too much time is poison for the atmosphere. The tension in a hackathon is great if the required result is demanding and the set time frame is tight. Lack of time acts like a pressure pot and the complexity of the task is the spice that makes each result individual.

In the following the common hackathon running times are described and tips for finding the right time and possible break arrangements are given.

2.2.1 The Short Hackathon

For participants who are very interested in the topic, 24 h is a manageable time. Here it is necessary to go a little beyond its normal limits. The willingness to participate is great. For the organizer it is sufficient to provide food and, if necessary, sleeping accommodations. But this is often not necessary, because the time is mostly used completely for development. However, although ideas can be expected during this period, fully implemented results are not realistic within this period of time. A presentation of results must be very much in the idea description. A deepening and concrete implementation, especially during a technology hackathon, cannot take place in this period. The advantage of this manageable time frame is the high level of interest and the actual desire to receive new impulses in a short time.

2.2.2 The Weekend Hackathon

The normal case for the length of a hackathon is about 48 h. Usually the hackathon starts around Friday afternoon and ends on Sunday between noon and afternoon. A hackathon over 2 days will provide you with better formulated results, first approaches to implementation, and also a more solid argumentation for business models and implementation plans.

For your hackathon, you will have to assess whether the task and possible solutions fill this time period and whether the participants are willing to invest this time. This depends on many factors. For example, material and cash prizes, jobs offered, or investors can be a good motivator.

2.2.3 The Very Long Hackathon

In order to obtain very detailed results, the period of implementation can also be significantly longer. Here, however, more emphasis is placed on virtual collaboration, the time for teamwork is freely allocated, and working in one place in different teams takes a back seat.

There are virtual hackathons which take place over half a year. The team members can be spread all over the world. The teams usually organize themselves with the help of online conferences, telephone, and cloud-based exchange services.

For such a hackathon, of course, completely different rules apply and the preparation and execution are drastically different from a normal hackathon. Here it is more important to motivate the teams to work together, to stimulate the permanent exchange, and to increase the long-term motivation. Of course, the character of the cooperation within the teams is also completely different, since in some cases the team members never met each other personally. In some cases there is an initial kick-off where everyone is present. The later elaboration then takes place separately again. Furthermore such a hackathon loses a lot of energy and speed compared to a normal hackathon because there is simply much more time available. This leads to more elaborate results, but also takes away a lot of the magic of the event.

So the final running time you decide on depends on many parameters. Normally you should plan (especially for your first hackathon) between 24 and 48 h.

2.2.4 The Smart Hackathon

Even a very short hackathon over a few hours can bring results. An idea generation process, perhaps even flanked by useful creativity techniques, can also find its place in a hackathon format without having to take days. In such short formats, the implementation will rather take a back seat due to lack of time. After only 4–8 h, the first results can be achieved. But expect here, just like in the short hackathon, no complex elaborations and extensive presentation and a working prototype. Rather, it is about using the creative energy of the competition idea to quickly develop new ideas, which can then be further elaborated afterwards and with more time.

2.2.5 The Right Date

Great care must be taken to avoid clashes of dates when scheduling each event. Negative effects can mean similar events in close proximity to each other, but semester breaks, school holidays, or bridge days can also have a negative effect on the number of registrations. If you would like to hold a hackathon within the scope of 1 or 2 days, the weekend is a good opportunity to organize an event. If you start on a Friday, you have to take into account not only the end of school or work but also the travel to the event. A start in the early evening is therefore pleasant and does not force participants to apply for holidays.

2.2.6 Pause Regulations

The essence of a hackathon is to work independently at your own pace. Pause rules should not be imposed from outside. Only the responsibility of the organizer for the health of the participants should be considered and an obvious self-overtaxation or overtiredness of individual participants may also lead to a direct approach to the persons concerned.

So during the work phase, make sure that the members of the organizing team and the coaches who are in direct contact with the participants constantly check how the teams are doing. You should also encourage breaks. During these breaks you should regularly eat, possibly sleep, or exercise (in the fresh air). Offer appropriate opportunities and activities. The final decision is of course up to the participants.

2.3   Legal Aspects

A hackathon event is from the view of the participants primarily an informal event. The mixture of professional challenge, fun in an unconventional leisure time activity, and perhaps also the interest in getting to know like-minded people promises at first a carefree contact with each other. However, the organizer must not encounter this carefree format guilelessly and under no circumstances unprepared. Clear rules make it easier for participants and the organizer to manage without real tension from the start to the end of the event.

It starts with the promotion of the event and can in some cases end with the exploitation rights of the results. However, considering these things beforehand and making binding agreements should not discourage potential participants. Therefore, the rules of the game must be agreed upon in a friendly, yet firm and perceptible manner. The following points cannot replace legal advice. In case of doubt, legal advice should always be sought for the individual project.

2.3.1   Proper Public Relations

A hackathon should be advertised intensively and early on. No matter if you decide to advertise on (university) pinboards, in specialist newspapers, on posters, on the internet, by mail, or by distributing flyers, there are a few things to consider.

The violation of image rights when creating advertising material does not seem so bad in view of an event that is only beneficial to all parties. But it still remains a copyright infringement. So when creating your marketing material, make sure you use properly licensed material or use special images and graphics that are provided free of charge for commercial use. There are corresponding portals on the internet that offer large collections of graphic material for free use. Conversely, a gray area may be to "recycle" proven event titles. At least a 1:1 copy of an event title can have legal repercussions in addition to the accusation of unimaginativeness, if the original inventor sees a claim to sole exploitation of any kind for himself.

Furthermore, when using partner names and their logos, make sure that you have written permission to do so. Many industrial companies continue to take great care to ensure that their names and logos are only displayed in the correct context, size, resolution, and color reproduction. Make sure that this is clearly agreed upon in advance. Unauthorized use can quickly lead to injunctions.

If you want to show photos or videos of previous hackathons in the invitation process, remember that you need the written permission of all persons depicted before you create this material. To ensure this, you should include a clause to that effect in the hackathon rules and have it signed during the registration process.

Basically, precaution is required. If you are not sure, it is better to ask a lawyer.

2.3.2   The Invitation Process

Inviting potential interested parties via e-mail is a quick and easy process. If the addressees and approaches are chosen correctly, a comparatively high response can be expected. The important thing here is to be able to find out how one came into possession of the e-mail addresses. While the use of e-mail crawlers still seemed to be permissible at the beginning of the twenty-first century, the European General Data Protection Regulation (GDPR) has contributed to the sensitive use of e-mail addresses and there are other strict regulations in different countries which have to be taken seriously. It is still possible, with explicit permission (the so-called opt-in procedure requires explicit consent, e.g. when creating a profile or confirming by button in a process). However, the purpose for which a person's e-mail address is used at the time of consent should also be sustainable. Even if in reality hardly any of those invited by e-mail will voice a complaint, one should always be aware of the currently applicable legal situation regarding the use of e-mail addresses and especially the threat of penalties.

Furthermore, you can also invite people whose data you already have by mail. A graphically nicely designed cover letter or a special card is something special and motivates to participate.

In addition to writing to people you already know, your goal can be to make new people aware of your hackathon. For this purpose, it is a good idea to create a homepage, announce the event, the motto, and the goals there, and then promote this page specifically via your social media channels.

The best way to do this is to create an invitation plan. In it, you should determine which channels you will use to address which target groups and when. This way you should start the address early and repeat the communication in several waves. This will ensure that your message is read and that latecomers, who may not have responded to the first message, still have a chance to participate in your hackathon.

Keep track of how many people have signed up and when. You may even be able to determine how people heard about the event. So you can evaluate afterwards which communication measures were the most successful and use this information for your next hackathon.

2.3.3   Media Accompaniment

Recordings at a hackathon create lasting impressions. As an organizer you want to take a lot of pictures and films. This requires clear agreements in advance or (if these have not been agreed upon) a careful execution. Since in most countries it is not allowed to take pictures of people from the front and in a recognizable way, one should also take precautions. In advance, an agreement in the conditions of participation can regulate that each participant gives his or her consent for film and photo shoots with his or her registration. Individual agreements with individual participants (recording of an interview, approved photos, etc.) are also possible.

If these agreements have not been made, shots from the front and the resulting recognition of the person are not permitted—as long as a subsequent written approval is not given.

Should you involve external media support, this must also be communicated in the rules in advance. Depending on your hackathon, the number of participants, and the importance of the event, it may also be that the press will be at the event. Clarify this in advance and, in the case of large events, offer appropriate accreditation and the provision of appropriate press material.

If you want to play commercial music at the event, you must remember to register your event to avoid rights infringements.

2.3.4 Agreement of Exploitation Rights

As a rule, a hackathon is organized by an economically stronger organizer, who in turn courts individuals, students, and small start-ups in a cooperative spirit. It is not a matter of course that the good ideas and results then belong to the organizer. It should be noted that there are two different interests at this point. The organizer wants to exploit the results of a hackathon in the form of good ideas from another. The participant will certainly see himself as the owner of an idea and thus the exploitation rights with himself. It is not intended to talk about patent law here nor to discuss the extent to which ideas can be an intangible economic good. Even if the creator of an idea is not yet of age and lives with his parents, the idea he came up with at a hackathon belongs to him. This also applies to a group of people who came up with an idea. One should think about exploitation rights in advance in ethical and legal terms. Even if one should be warned against over-regulation, clear agreements in the conditions of participation can avoid problems. One such rule could be, for example, that a hackathon idea is compensated with the award of a material or monetary prize and the exploitation rights are transferred to the organizer.

Remaining unclear involves many dangers:

- Ideas are not exploited because there is a dispute about exploitability.
- An idea is exploited by one side, the other side disagrees.
- A third party takes possession of the idea because none of the brawlers dares to exploit it.
- Participating start-ups feel deprived of an idea because the hackathon rules expropriate the start-up of your idea via the terms and conditions of participation.

If you become uncertain about the participation of certain applicants, communication with the applicant is the recommended means.

A special case here is surely internal hackathons. If new ideas are generated here, it is highly likely that this will happen on the basis of the knowledge conveyed in advance at company expense and also during working hours. In this case, it is particularly important to ensure that the motivation still arises and that employees feel compelled to develop their ideas further. Here, cash and material prizes as well as honestly meant awards can be the right means.

A second special case, which arises by agreement, is the assignment of the exploitation rights to a sponsor, who as the financial sponsor of the hackathon has options for exploitation rights. This form of implementation has to be documented extensively and has to be transparent towards the participants.

The third case in dealing with exploitation rights is the agreement that basically no ideas worthy of protection will result from the hackathon. This should not be a "first come, first served" approach, but it is up to the process within the hackathon to simply ensure that the correct handling of results is fair.

In any case, a clear and open presentation of the arrangements made must be communicated to all participants in advance. It is best to include the rules directly in the registration process. Therefore all participants must read them and agree to them by signing the registration form.

It should be noted that many participants are deterred by too strict rules and the complete abandonment of the right to their own idea and possibly stay away from the hackathon. In any case this has to be taken into consideration.

2.3.5 Exclusion Criteria

The diversity among the hackathon participants is usually an important ingredient for the really good and newly conceived results of such a competition. Interdisciplinary participants are almost always a good idea and only in exceptional cases should participants be explicitly excluded via the rules. In particular, if participants obviously have no prospect of meaningful participation, for example, due to lack of expertise or a complete lack of language skills, participation should at least be questioned. But also a violation of "equality of arms" in the other direction makes participation in a hackathon rather difficult. Start-ups in a team and professionals who have been in the profession for a long time and have proven special knowledge in the hackathon topic are typical candidates who would prevent the comparability of the creative results in a hackathon. Exclusion criteria should always be chosen with care because the feeling of having set up discriminatory rules can be very much a part of a hackathon.

2.3.6 Fraudulent Intentions

The prize money of a hackathon also tempts participants to simply fall back on proven methods in the jungle of the multi-faceted and unmanageable world of innovation. It is dishonorable and also fraudulent to be awarded a prize in a hackathon for an idea that has already been conceived. Unfortunately, it is common in sports and hackathons alike to cheat honest players out of their fame. Apart from stealing ideas, another form of cheating is working with helpers who are not on site. In IT hackathons, participants regularly work with their own laptops and unlimited Internet access. This also allows them to work with an unlimited team of virtual participants connected via chat and e-mail. This form of cheating should be outlawed by a very specific reference in the terms and conditions of participation and corresponding participants or even entire teams should be expelled if they fail to comply with the competition.

However, the risk cannot be completely controlled. To uncover a fraud after the event is very unpleasant—it takes the shine off the whole event retroactively. Therefore, comparable to the doping test in a hackathon, the measure is limited to the period between the end of the hackathon and the awarding of the prize. Here the extended jury can find out by internet research whether the submitted idea has been cribbed. To prevent communication with external parties in a hackathon is unthinkable due to the many different communication possibilities alone.

2.3.7 Regulations

In case of large and externally conducted hackathons, a corresponding permission to conduct an event must usually be obtained from the respective responsible office. Under certain circumstances, conditions may be imposed which must be implemented. These include, for example, fire protection regulations, provision of medical and security personnel, and noise regulations. There are no standards here and each country, federal state, and each municipality can regulate this differently. Please inquire early enough and adhere strictly to the given regulations, otherwise the event may be canceled.

2.3.8 Other Rules

All rules that participants must follow when participating should be laid down and made known. This can include a ban on drugs and alcohol as well as the prohibition of loud music during the hackathon. Individually, an organizer should establish guidelines within the framework of the house rules, as long as these are not pointless, unfulfillable, or a motivation killer.

Furthermore, you should set up rules for fair dealing with each other, which the participants must adhere to. In most cases this is not a problem at hackathons. But in intense discussions, especially towards the end of the hackathon, things can get a bit heated. Here no discussions should be stopped, but they should be fought out objectively and without threats, insults, and above all without physical violence. Such disregard should be reminded promptly and should lead to exclusion in case of violation.

2.4   Advertising

Once the desired number of participants and thus the size of a hackathon have been determined, appropriate measures will be taken to ensure that enough registrations are received. But the addressees of such an advertisement are equally people who see this as a great action, who are interested in a job in this organization, who want to acquire venture capital, or who are simply interested in following the life in your city. Nerds, founders, students but also pupils and working people can be part of the target group and this should be considered when applying and choosing the advertising channels.

In the following we will explain the topic of hackathon advertising and the respective design in more detail.

2.4.1   Name and Motto of the Event

The recognition value of a hackathon is significantly linked to its name. Unconsumed, clear, and creative, the name of a hackathon can become a trademark that can be used and reused for years. The name of a hackathon can be a combination of several words, if this gives more information about the goal of the hackathon. Since a catchy name usually cannot convey the meaning and purpose of a hackathon, a subtitle may be used. If this subtitle is catchy and represents the motto at the same time, a lot is gained. It is not necessary and rather advantageous that the word hackathon appears in the name or motto. Not every interested person may know what to do with the term hackathon and so the first thing to do is to gain attention and send a positive invitation. Superlatives should be avoided as well as very commercial titles. The subtitle or the motto of the hackathon should give an interested person an idea at first hearing whether it is worthwhile to get more information about this event and to read on. If you also want to give the eye an anchor point and increase the recognition value, you may consider creating your own logo. If one considers this, please use a professionally designed logo. A self-made logo is usually recognizable as such and can stand in the way of the desire to leave a professional impression.

What you should not reveal before the start of the hackathon is the exact task. This will only be announced with the start of the hackathon. Otherwise there is a danger that too much preparatory work will be done by teams and a competition-distorting situation will arise. In addition, a preliminary information would draw one of the most exciting moments (the announcement of the actual task) before the hackathon.

So use the invitation to build up a positive tension and motivate the participants in such a way that they want to participate, although it is not yet clear what it will be about in concrete terms.

2.4.2 Website

A hackathon should not be a minor matter and so an announcement on your own website is also necessary. This possibility is mostly cost-neutral and can also be connected with a central registration link. Also an own website for the organization of a hackathon should be considered. This again underlines the importance of the hackathon and also allows completely individual design elements. The following information should at least be listed:

- Title and motto of the hackathon
- Date, duration, and location of the event
- Which potential participants are addressed?
- What is there to win and according to which criteria are prizes awarded?
- What to bring, what to get locally?
- A way to ask questions up front
- A registration link with a reference to compliance with the data protection guidelines and other regulations

2.4.3 Advertising in Trade Journals or Local Press

Local daily newspapers are interested in news and events. A note to the editorial office is quickly done and this form of advertising is cost-neutral. However, if you want to attract attention beyond local borders, it makes sense to publish the announcement in trade journals 3 months in advance. However, the costs incurred for this can be considerable.

2.4.4 Flyer, Poster, Printed Matter

A regionally limited hackathon on a university campus, for example, or within a company can also be successfully advertised with classic print material. You can, for example, use flyers and posters. This form of advertising is inexpensive and printed material offers the advantage that paper also has a reminder function.

2.4.5 E-Mailing and Viral Marketing

The use of address lists for direct invitations via e-mail is effective and inexpensive. Legal aspects have already been referred to in Sect. 2.3.2. The use of social media channels offers almost unlimited reach. However, the flood of information on the internet also offers a risk of being overlooked at a large number of events.

2.4.6 Word of Mouth

Free of charge and very successful is the direct approach to exactly those target groups that you would like to see at your event. This can be done very directly and a phone call with a reference to the event will not offend anyone. Use your network (and that of your colleagues) and personally activate as many people as possible. A recommendation among friends is worth much more than simple advertising. This should fill your list of participants quickly.

2.4.7 Media Partnership

If there are trade journals or even publishing houses that have a close connection to the hackathon topic, the agreement of a media partnership should be considered. This should be discussed at a very early stage. The advantages of such an agreement are obvious:

- Consistent reporting at all stages of the hackathon implementation
- Reaching the respective target group in print and online media
- Coordinated media mix on the previously mentioned advertising possibilities

2.4.8 Live Reporting

It is in keeping with the spirit of the times that the successful progress of the event is also reported in real time on social networks. Whether pictures, statements of the participants, or even interim results are reported here is up to the organizer. It is important that the spontaneous reporting via Facebook, Twitter, etc. is also quality-assured and that the guidelines on data protection, right to one's own picture, etc. are observed. Profiles in social networks especially for use during the hackathon can also be used in advance to promote the event. Offering a live stream of the event on the internet is undoubtedly a highlight, but requires an announcement to the participants and their consent in advance.

2.5 Venue

The goal of every organizer should be to make the hackathon an unforgettable event. But since not only beautiful pictures should remain in the minds of the participants of a hackathon, but also the environment should be captured in photo-documentary form for press and own use, a certain demand should be made on the venue. The aspects of suitable infrastructure in terms of sufficient food, retreats, washing facilities, and also sleeping places become more important the longer a hackathon is to last.

In the following the choice of the right location is described in more detail.

2.5.1 The Ideal Location

If it is not a regionally limited hackathon, metropolises with good transport infrastructure and long-distance train stations are preferable to rural regions. The special nature of a hackathon naturally allows for exceptions.

At the location of a hackathon one spends a lot of time. You should be able to feel comfortable there. Hackathons basically offer moments that are meant for everyone and thus a large number of people in one room, but they also need the location for retreat, concentration, discussion, and recharging their batteries. Therefore, hotels with large halls and many small retreat rooms are never a wrong choice. But this environment is also much cheaper in universities. If comparable conditions are also offered in locations that are well known regionally or nationally and they have a certain extravagance or are simply surprising, then these can also be taken into account because these locations can add a special flair to the event.

In the following, the concrete planning of the premises with its individual aspects will be discussed.

2.5.2 A Sensible Spatial Division

Most space is needed by the plenum and thus the area where organizers, helpers, and above all participants come together. This is where the welcoming, the award ceremony at the end, and in between the development will take place. It makes sense that the persons who are to serve as a central contact person are also located here. In a central place there should also be a material store with multiple sockets, extension cables, paper, pens, plasters, handkerchiefs, screwdrivers, and adhesive tape. Depending on the nature of the hackathon, these can be completely different things and tools. The central area must be bright, spacious, and well air-conditioned. Areas in which intensive work is done, where teams discuss or even rest should be designable. Whether the table is used for sleeping or the sofa for working can be left up to the participants. The locations should be close together. The noise level should be bearable over the period of the event. Because there will be announcements by the organizers before, during, and after the actual hackathon work phase, a stage or a raised place should be available, from which central speeches like welcome, organizational information but also the farewell can be held.

Furthermore make sure that a sufficient number of toilets and washrooms are available. These will be heavily frequented, especially before (sleeping) breaks and in the morning hours, and should be distributed throughout the building and be easily accessible. Pay particular attention to a high cleaning frequency in these rooms and plan for appropriate personnel.

In order to facilitate navigation in the building, you should provide all participants with an appropriate site plan when registering and also provide extensive signposting in the building.

2.5.3 The Service Desk

Every hackathon participant will come across questions during the course of the event. These are manifold and not always foreseeable. Maybe simple things of daily use are missing like a paper clip, a pen, or someone who wants the menu of a pizza service. You should be prepared for this.

It is best to prepare a central point of contact at a central location or in the reception room, which should be manned at all times. If it cannot be a place with a table and one person, then you should set up a telephone number, a WhatsApp address, or a bulletin board with question options. This place will be heavily frequented at the beginning of a hackathon, less in between, and more towards the end of the hackathon.

The topic of technical support is also very important. Here it is about WLAN and other network connections, power supply, and connections of further devices like projectors and music systems. For technically designed hackathons in which, for example, soldering and working with 3D-printers is to be done, you also have to provide equipment, spare parts, and a safe operation. All in all, it is a good idea to have a technical support team that can take care of the event from planning to implementation and act as a contact person and "rapid reaction force" on site. Make sure that the team is known and always available (for example, via the service desk).

2.5.4 What Else Is to Be Thought of?

Adequate and free catering is part of being a good host. Drinks quickly become a bottleneck and should therefore never be underestimated during the entire duration of a hackathon. In addition to the provision of water and normal cold drinks, the organizer is also given the opportunity at this point to select the "energy drinks" responsibly. Strongly sugary drinks do not always have to be the first choice. Tea, coffee, and mate drinks can complement this. Every 6 h a kind of main course should be offered, i.e. breakfast, lunch, and dinner. During the whole time fruit and in small quantities gum, chocolate, liquorice, or similar are very good idea.

It is a good idea to use a local catering service for the supply. They can also provide appropriate personnel, in which case you do not have to take care of this point yourself. To what extent paramedics are needed is at the discretion of the organizer. Although neither alcohol poisoning nor brawls are to be expected at hackathons, the physical and mental strain over a long period of time should not be underestimated. In any case, the possible case of acute need for medical help should be considered in advance. In this context it is also advisable to have sleeping places, beanbags, and perhaps even blankets available. The latter, as the temperature and air conditioning are almost always questioned by participants and at least very differently assessed.

2.5.5 Special Case: Online Hackathon

All the above-mentioned aspects lose their validity in the case of the special format online hackathon. Here, the focus is not on spatial gathering, but rather on the possibility for participants from all over the world to work virtually on a hackathon task. Besides the obvious advantages and also cost savings, there are also disadvantages. Getting to know each other, building up a sense of "togetherness," experiencing and enduring the stress are not possible online. Also the working method, composition of the teams, and adherence to rules are difficult to grasp. The technical effort and also the requirements on the participant side are considerably higher in an online hackathon. Therefore this special format of a hackathon will not be given further attention in this book.

2.6 Equipment and Technology

Although the hackathon event format is not limited to the digitization sector, it is very often represented here. Therefore special attention must be paid to this topic. At no event everything will run smoothly all the time, but anticipating and being prepared is what makes for good organization. Even non-technical hackathons need infrastructure, electricity, and almost always WLAN access.

The following chapters will show you what needs to be prepared in detail.

2.6.1 Own or Loaned Equipment

If you would like to offer an all-round service or simply increase equal opportunities, notebooks can be provided in sufficient quantities. Without a hardware sponsor, however, this can represent a further cost block. However, it does provide opportunities to offer preconfigured software and peripherals and thus standardize the infrastructure used. It is even possible to prevent access to external networks and, if desired, to limit connectivity to the outside world (for example, to limit shadow team building). The BYOD (Bring Your Own Device, see [6]) approach, however, is most often encountered in practice and offers the team member the highest productivity.

2.6.2 WLAN and Adequate Connectivity

A WLAN access for each participant is assumed as a matter of course. Although there are no extended liability risks on the part of the organizer, a well-secured network should be offered in the interest of the participants. WLAN coverage of the central event location is just as important as that of the places where the participants work, research, or perhaps communicate. Here the existing systems are often not sufficient. Check the location in advance for network coverage and, if in doubt, temporarily expand the WLAN infrastructure by adding more routers or repeaters.

The requirement of equal opportunities means that the same access to the mobile network is also roughly equal. In addition to network availability and local connectivity, pay attention to the available bandwidth. Remember that many people are simultaneously on the internet via a central line and potentially exchange data with each other. Here the location must offer sufficient capacity for network access. If in doubt, additional bandwidth must be purchased from the network provider for the duration of the event.

Please note that you must set up rules for the use of the network access provided and have these confirmed in writing by each participant as part of the registration. The rules should, in their minimal form, restrict use to legal services and internet sites. Further rules depend on the type and scope of your hackathon and should be added individually.

2.6.3 Periphery

The technical periphery and equipment must be available, hardly needs to be mentioned. It is much more important that things are available in sufficient quantity and that they work. The devil is often in the details and one is well advised to keep things in stock in excess rather than having to organize them later under time pressure. These things do not have to be bought, but can usually be borrowed with a little creativity.

- Printers should be fast and have WLAN capability.
- The final presentation on the projector should be possible for every participant.
- Many hours at a technical console require sufficiently large monitors.
- Power strips should be available in sufficient quantity, as well as extension cables and tape to fix the cables.
- Adapter to the projector or to monitors, as well as spare power supplies if necessary should be available in sufficient quantities.
- Keep a sufficient number of USB sticks or mobile hard disks in a central location for fast transfer of large amounts of data.
- The luxury equipment includes laser pointers, presentation clickers, computer mice, and keyboards.

2.6.4 Platform and Cloud Access

Today, a technical infrastructure can be provided almost completely from a cloud infrastructure in the case of hackathons that are very technology-heavy. For this purpose, manufacturers also offer free test accesses, which can often be used free of charge for several weeks. A particular advantage is that interim results from the hackathon can be further developed and used afterwards. With this variant, it is advisable for participants to receive access to a cloud instance ahead of time.

2.6.5 Licenses

Attention must be paid throughout the entire event to the observance of third-party rights, in particular trademark rights and licensing rights. Test licenses are often a cost-neutral option, but subscriptions with an obligation to cancel should not be taken out.

As part of the general rules, point out to all participants in advance that only legally licensed or free software may be used. Make sure that all participants accept and confirm this point in writing during registration. In this way, you will remove yourself from possible liability.

2.6.6 Consumables

Depending on the theme and type of the hackathon, it is also the responsibility of the organizer to provide sufficient consumables for all teams. In an artistic hackathon this can be canvas, paint, and brushes. In a technology hackathon it can be technical building blocks and soldering stations and in other hackathon formats completely different tools and consumables. Apart from sufficient quantity, sufficient quality must also be ensured. Furthermore, for reasons of fairness, make sure that all teams receive the same materials in the same quantity.

2.6.7 Analog Resources

The need for paper, pens, and other classic aids such as sticky notes is often underestimated. Since this is not a very relevant cost item, generous planning should be made here. Presentation cases and whiteboards do not have to be bought, but should not be borrowed at the last minute. In the course of equal treatment, a sufficient number of aids should be available for everyone. For a hackathon outside the technology sector, analogous aids are also materials, tools, and consumables. A little bell, a pipe, or a similar instrument to attract attention is a small but very effective aid when the expected noise level is high.

2.7 The Organizing Team

Hackathons can inspire a lot of people, but someone also has to take care of planning, execution, and follow-up. Own staff, staff of co-organizers, and even family members are regularly the people who bear the main burden of implementation.

The important resource human being is therefore not only on the participant side part of a successful hackathon. Therefore, it is recommended to set up the organizer team described below at a very early stage. Apart from a blocker in the schedule, everyone in the organizer team must be aware of the importance of their role in the process at an early stage.

2.7.1   The Planning Staff

The core team of an event is the group of people who will be responsible for content, budget, procedure, and media support. A serious hackathon is an important event for any organization, so planning should also be a matter for the boss. Again, the more different functions are linked to the people, the more likely it is that all aspects will be sufficiently considered and appreciated. In addition to those responsible for marketing, the planning team should include people with a high level of expertise. As in the teams described below, functionaries who are particularly critical to success should always be provided with a substitute regulation.

2.7.2   Supervisors

The most important analogous means are the organizers themselves, who should at any time intensively take care of the participants. Recruiting experts who can take the same strain as hackathon participants—as part of your work and as an extra mile—requires a lot of preparation. These coaches must be willing to work on weekends, to work unconventionally, and to face a long working time. Therefore, the enthusiasm of these helpers must be as great as that of the participants themselves. The more specialized the topic of the hackathon was called, the more the selection of these people can be a bottleneck. It is important that over the long period of a hackathon, people from the planning team are always present. Very specific questions, unexpected wishes, or criticism, to which quick reactions are required, can often only be assessed by the planning team itself.

2.7.3   Mentors

Mentors, who as part of the organizer team take care of the teams from the beginning of the event, answer questions, give suggestions, and provide motivation, are key to the event. Whether a mentor accompanies one or more teams will be decided by the number of available mentors. However, mentors must not distort competition or become the decisive driving force of the event, but should as a catalyst in the team promote a successful implementation of ideas.

2.7.4 Moderator

At least one person is to be provided as moderator, who explains the course of events before the hackathon, makes interim announcements, and always brings structure in the choreography of the event. This person is automatically considered to be the contact person and should therefore be closely involved in the organization. The way of moderation can be done in the style of a conférencier with a light humorous touch.

2.8 Costs

The realization of an event always requires a financial budget in addition to some personnel expenditure. However, planning rarely works out exactly and even less often you need less budget than you thought. For this reason, a buffer of around 10% is always recommended, which is available for contingencies that are certain to occur. The cost blocks are described in the following according to the presumed shares in descending order.

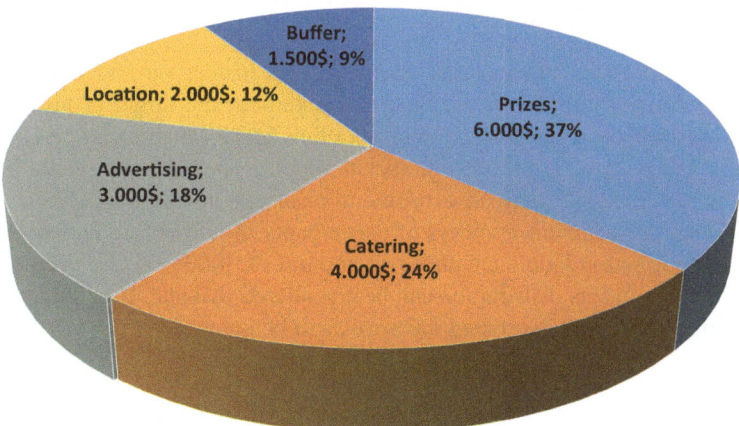

Fig. 2.2 Example calculation for a hackathon with 80 participants

Figure 2.2 shows a sample calculation for a hackathon with 80 participants.

2.8.1 Prize Money

From the participants' point of view the attractiveness of a hackathon increases with the amount of prize money. Since there should be at least three staggered winning classes (first, second, and third), a considerably sum is quickly added up here. For a hackathon with 80 participants we assume prizes worth 3000$ (first prize), 2000$

(second prize), and 1000$ (third prize). Even if a hackathon is based on material prizes, these are directly quantifiable in monetary terms.

2.8.2 Catering

The event format of a hackathon aims to allow participants to work through the event undisturbed over a longer period of time. It does not make sense to send the participants outside of the event in search of food, nor would this be a sign of good host qualities. Rather, a full service should be included in the calculation. You can certainly save money by preparing your own meals or by using prepackaged food—but appreciation of the participants through good catering always has a motivational effect. You should definitely plan on 50$–80$ per person and day. A large part of the costs will be for drinks. If the event location is connected with an obligation to purchase, e.g. by the hotel or landlord, the costs can be higher. However, in this case you often have the advantage of being able to fall back on empirical values and a proven calculation. We calculate 4000$ food costs for an 80-participant hackathon.

2.8.3 Advertising

The costs that are spent to increase attention to a hackathon and thus to attract participants depend largely on the type of hackathon, the target groups, and the attention. A spatially limited hackathon on a university campus can be advertised with flyers and posters; a nationwide hackathon on a special topic would be more likely to be advertised through advertisements or inserts in magazines. Basically the effort to generate sufficient numbers of participants should not be underestimated. If we assume a nationwide hackathon, an amount of 3000$ for the printing of an advertising flyer and its distribution can be considered realistic. In reality, however, several complementary advertising measures will be launched.

2.8.4 Premises

The costs incurred with regard to premises to be rented can also vary considerably. University rooms can be rented at a relatively low price. An event in a hotel, however, will be much more cost-intensive. In the latter case, it is not always possible to separate the costs for food and rooms. As a general rule, the more unusual the venue is chosen, the more likely it is that a noticeable block of costs will be incurred. A basic amount of 2000$ should be realistic and rather conservative.

2.8.5   Agency Services

Many organizers use an agency to make use of their professionalism in the invitation process, communication, or concept development. Even the entire operation of a hackathon as a "hackathon as a service" can be commissioned nowadays. In this case, however, only an accompanying role of an agency should be included in the cost consideration. These companies usually require a certain minimum commitment. A realistic estimate of around 2000$ is to be made here. However, the main responsibility in the planning process should lie with the organizer's team, and agencies can be seen as an extended workbench.

2.8.6   Technology, Loan, Licenses

Smaller items can be omitted for the provision of technical infrastructure. Whether it is borrowing a projector, setting up a hotspot, using a specific software package, or the fee for musical background accompaniment—smaller items will be incurred. A buffer is required for precisely these smaller and difficult to plan positions. From this buffer, smaller material resources from the power strip to paper and other unforeseen procurements can also be made. Here, a total of 10% of the calculated costs can be added to the sum of the calculated costs in order to keep an adequate buffer.

2.9   Sponsors

It would be a fine art of a hackathon organizer if he could allocate all his costs to sponsors. In reality, there will be a mixture between an own budget as basis and various contributions from sponsors or co-organizers. Although these contributions may include not only money, but also manpower in the form of assistance and material resources, the focus here is primarily on money.

2.9.1   Sponsor Selection

The choice of sponsors determines a substantial part of the external perception of a hackathon, grants rights of co-determination or, for example, gives a technical direction. In the first case, the event can be presented in a dynamic and modern light, with a beverage manufacturer providing the cold or energy drinks and thus advertising itself. A sponsor, on the one hand, who contributes funds and pursues similar goals to yourself, is more likely to be a partner with a corresponding say. On the other hand, if a partner provides a technical device or platform in a hackathon, he or she will give the event a predetermined choice of technology. With all these possible approaches, the most important thing is that the individual sponsors complement each other, do not compete and see themselves as team players.

2.9.2 Sponsor Packages

In addition to advertising space and visibility, co-organizers also demand participation with regard to the goals pursued, in the implementation and would certainly like to have a say in the awarding of prizes for the best ideas. To ensure that the intensity of participation and co-determination is fair and does not amount to haggling, it is advisable to describe the sponsorship rules in advance. Sponsorship packages (e.g. platinum, gold, silver) have proven their worth here, which contrast the performance and thus the financial contribution made with a correspondingly graded right to a say and also graded visibility. It is advisable here to determine very precisely what a sponsor receives in return for his contribution, as this way, ambiguities during the actual implementation do not become a disruptive factor.

The dimensions of sponsor expectations are at least the following:

- Visibility in the invitation process and a mention as co-organizer
- Advertising opportunity at the event
- Participation in the jury to select the best solution
- Share of the exploitation rights of the solutions devised

2.9.3 Sponsors

The sponsor benefits are essentially money. However, since not only money leads to a successful hackathon, but the entire package that a sponsor brings in, the material assets, material prizes, technology provided for use, but above all a proportionate amount of work in preparation and support should be taken into consideration. As soon as more than two sponsors are involved, sensitivities should be counteracted. This works best if all contributions in kind (e.g. material prize costs 3000$) are clearly evaluated, but above all the work of each sponsor, e.g. by looking after the participants over 24 h, is evaluated in monetary terms (e.g. 24 h with two experts at 30$ per hour approx. 1500$). It is somewhat more difficult in cases where a sponsor provides, e.g. his technology—here he incurs costs, but at the same time he has generated an advertising effect. But here, too, the following applies: What was discussed beforehand does not lead to ambiguity later.

2.10 Prices and Incentives

The attractiveness of a hackathon is determined by the topic, the fun factor but also by a promising reward. This enumeration also reflects the correct order of motivation among hackathon participants. The prize money should not be astronomical and the motivation through content and fun should be in the foreground. Intangible prizes are attractive and should not be underestimated.

In the following, the individual prize categories are presented in detail.

2.10.1 Cash Prizes

Those who bring a lot of know-how with them, but do not yet have an adequate salary or have been waiting for a chance to have their idea rewarded at least once, will see a high incentive in cash prizes and will participate in a hackathon with commitment. For people who already have a secure and adequate income, the amount of prize money will only increase the attractiveness of a hackathon. On the part of the participants the chance of a high prize money in a hackathon can be increased by a professionalized approach. High prize money therefore attracts hackathon professionals. However, the essence of a hackathon is characterized by equal opportunities, a little altruism, and the desire for a large number of participants. Six-figure prize money is already common in the USA—and here a professional image of the hackathon participant is slowly developing. This development is to be rejected and a prize money should only be an incentive for each participant. As organizer one does well to follow the value-oriented idea of the Olympic Games—great attention, many winners, and being there is everything. Therefore cash prizes are only one ingredient in the motivation cocktail.

2.10.2 Material Prizes

Material prices are a good advertising space if they are anyway related to the business area or environment of the organizer. If a manufacturer in the technology industry organizes a hackathon, a number of sponsored articles as prizes are a suitable form of incentive. Very small non-cash prizes as so-called giveaways are suitable to give every hackathon participant a minimal promise of winning in advance and also to ensure that no one is released from a hackathon without a reward. If material prizes are also unique, e.g. because it is a limited product, or an engraving makes the prize unique, then the actual material value is also linked to an ideal value. It is not wrong to offer a prize for the teams of a hackathon, but it usually leads to its liquidation on a sales platform due to a lack of divisibility. It is seldom possible to offer a valuable prize for each member of a winning team, as the size of the teams and thus the costs associated with prizes are not predictable. It is not a good idea to prohibit the resale of non-cash prizes because the organizer rarely benefits from this and participants are prevented from making the best possible use of the prize.

2.10.3 Intangible Prizes

Intangible prices are allowed, if they are actually of value to the participants. A license for a software which in the end has little relevance for the participant or an internship as a prize for an experienced professional in permanent employment may disappoint the award winners. Therefore, a sense of proportion should be applied not only when selecting the prizes, but even more so when selecting the prize winners. Here the jury is welcome to take a subjective view in the evaluation process, if it serves the satisfaction of the award winners in the end. Intangible prizes have the potential to express special appreciation. This can be expressed in an internship for job starters, the free use of a software or platform license for all participants, but also a certificate with corresponding appreciation represents a value for participants and winners.

2.10.4 Venture Capital

Funds for the business implementation of one's own idea (the so-called venture capital (VC)) are in great demand in the start-up scene. For the organizer, VC means a high degree of confidence in the idea of the hackathon prize winner, and at the same time a sum of at least five figures as an investment in a new, previously unknown business partner. However, not every hackathon participant is interested in VC. A hackathon that offers prizes in the form of VC is therefore only interesting for participants from the start-up scene. VC can, however, be offered to selected participants independently of the actual evaluation regulations. The complexity of the VC assignment and corresponding pre-contractual regulations can thus be taken from the actual hackathon event.

2.10.5 Cooperation, Internships, and Employment

Similar to the VC aspect, the topic of future cooperation, internships, and employment in the company can be offered to participants. However, these things are unsuitable as a price, as they can never be a unilateral legal transaction. Nevertheless, such offers are very welcome by the participants. While even the awarding of a prize in the sense of a gift is a two-sided legal transaction, the arrangements for the above-mentioned topics require detailed agreements and contractual bases. These cannot realistically be made in the run-up to the hackathon, but are recommended as a productive epilogue to every hackathon. The initiation of such extended cooperation approaches often takes place during the work phase of the hackathon.

If you are thinking about a hackathon as a recruiting instrument, you should involve your human resources department at an early stage. Clarify which profiles are currently being searched for and what requirements are made of the new people to be recruited. During the hackathon, HR staff should also be on site to answer questions, advertise the company, and potentially conduct direct (short) job interviews.

After the hackathon, more in-depth interviews with interested participants can be planned.

2.11 Jury, Presentation, and Award Ceremony

At the end of each hackathon the best ideas are awarded and the prizes are presented. This phase should not take much longer than one and a half hours after the official end of the hackathon work and the creative phase. All participants have many hours of concentration and teamwork behind them. The impatience and desire to enter the recovery phase will be present in almost every active participant and the organizer. The teams that do not belong to the winners should be given as much attention as the winners themselves. Every participant and every team that has survived a hackathon deserves respect and an appreciation of their performance. This should also be done on a big stage.

In the next chapters the different aspects of preparing for the end of the hackathon will be described in detail.

2.11.1 Composition of the Jury

A high-ranking jury, which apart from the evaluation of the achievements also takes over the task of the award, means large appreciation for the participants. Conversely, however, the expertise and high level of expertise in the jury are to be rated even higher. A comprehensible and fair evaluation of the presentations and performances presented represents a round and conciliatory conclusion of the event even for the non-award winners. The jury can be recruited from the ranks of the organizers. In order to maintain its independence, a jury may also be composed entirely of external experts or dignitaries. Even if the jury members are to be found at different hierarchical levels in real life, there must be an absolute equality of votes within the jury.

2.11.2 Task of the Jury

The advice of the jury must be fast and well organized. If certificates are issued, they must be issued at the same time as the deliberations or immediately afterwards, so that team names, participant names, scores, and signatures can be handed over directly for the awards. The jury should not only carry out the awarding of prizes itself, but should also briefly explain and justify why the performances of the winning teams should be rated higher than those of the others. It would also be a nice touch for the jury if you could also briefly mention the non-award winners and their performance in one or two sentences in appreciation. The order in which the prizes are awarded should be enough to create a sense of suspense and lead from the rear places to the front. In order for the jury's work to function well, the jury members should not get to know each other only at the time of the jury evaluation, but should be familiar with each other beforehand. In this case, the awarding of the prizes can also be carried out jointly and coordinated by all jury members in front of an audience.

2.11.3 Size of the Jury

An uneven number of jury members prevents the effect of a tie vote. Too many jury members increase the voting effort in the evaluation process. A jury that is too small may have too little ability to evaluate. A jury of five or seven people may be considered favorable.

2.11.4 Evaluation Criteria and Jury Rules

If the essence of a hackathon is the thinking of the "unthought," the refinement, and rudimentary implementation of an idea, then the presentation itself should be given the least weight. In this way, too much emphasis would be placed on the professionalism, age, and rhetorical maturity of the teams. Instead, the evaluation should be based on the idea and its implementation. The following evaluation criteria could be a benchmark:

- Uniqueness of the idea (25%)
- Practicality (25%)
- Benefits and social relevance (25%)
- Approach and quality of implementation (25%)

Of course, other evaluation criteria with different weightings are also conceivable. It is important that these criteria are already known to the participants in advance and that the teams have the opportunity to adjust to these evaluation priorities. Practically, each jury member will be given notes in advance, on which these criteria are already noted and which should serve for easier and quicker evaluation. On the basis of these criteria, the jury is to exchange arguments and make assessments. Within these criteria, the use of a clear evaluation scale (e.g. school grades A/1 [corresponds to very good], F/6 [corresponds to very bad]) is recommended. These values in relation to your weighting will result in a total score per team, which should be a quite objective measure for the performance of the teams.

2.12   Alternative: Special Prize

Maybe teams are not comfortable with the task presented at the beginning of the hackathon, but still want to participate. Or maybe the organizer wants to achieve a nuance or emphasis of a certain problem besides the central hackathon theme. In such cases a special price can be considered, which is to be appreciated in its meaning also with attention. Here a parallel track to the actual hackathon theme could be opened. Apart from more freedom, other rules for implementation and more artistic freedom could also apply here. So also teams with ideas can get a chance, which do not quite correspond to the hackathon task with a great idea, but would like to work out a valuable contribution to the theme environment.

2.13 Supporting Program

A successful hackathon may well be a colorful event, which, in addition to the actual competition, may also offer opportunities for diversion. At the so-called side events manifold information can flow, conversations can be held, experiences can be made possible, or people can be brought into contact. Not too many side events should be offered at the same time, as this is distracting and time-consuming.

2.13.1 Presentation of the Organizers

Participants in a hackathon often hope to learn more about the organizer in his role as a potential employer. The organizers themselves often see a hackathon as an opportunity to present themselves as an innovative employer. The resulting synergy can be well planned in advance in a hackathon. A small information stand can be the starting point for information material on the organization, the professional fields, and current vacancies. This contact point should be positioned somewhat more quietly to allow confidential and undisturbed discussions and should be accessible during the entire time of the event.

2.13.2 Exhibits and World of Experience

If the organizer has interesting objects of his work focus, new products or new research results to show, these may serve as a supporting program at the side of the actual event. Besides the possibility to inform, there may also be a possibility for self-promotion or simply a chance for a conversation.

2.13.3 Discussion Forums

When interested parties and experts come together on a specific topic, there are always discussions and a lively exchange of views. In order for this to take place in an organized form, at a specific time and place, a discussion forum can be planned as a supporting program. This has the advantage that the organizer can take over the control of the targeted exchange and that all participants can participate and benefit equally.

2.13.4 Podium

The refined version of the discussion forum can be a discussion group organized with predetermined persons. A discourse led by a moderator, determined by the topic and of finite length, can have a stimulating effect on such a circle. Placed at the beginning of the hackathon, participants can also be given further ideas, get to know other perspectives, and delve into a topic.

2.14   Creative Additions

The uniqueness of a hackathon event results from the sum of its parts. Thus, a raffle, surprise moments, live cooking, a food truck, or event illustrators can also be used as a framework. There are no limits to your creativity. But please note that the focus is on the actual hackathon and the implementation of the projects. Everything else is a decorative accessory. But it is this very accessory that can make the difference in a hackathon.

2.15   Summary

- The preparation phase is by far the longest and busiest time in the implementation of your hackathon.
- A planning time of several months for the preparation of a hackathon cannot be avoided.
- Plan all important aspects in advance and be prepared for deviations from the plan. This allows you to react flexibly during the event.
- Clarify the expectations of all organizers and sponsors of the hackathon in advance. This will help you avoid disappointment.
- The backbone of a successful hackathon is a motivated and enthusiastic organization team.
- The devil is in the details and therefore one should work intensively with checklists.
- Transparency in external and internal communication is critical to success.
- A hackathon is (just like all other events) subject to legal regulations. Please consider these regulations already during the planning stage and especially emphasize data protection and the handling of intellectual property. Get legal support to be on the safe side.

Operation

3

Abstract

The actual operation of your hackathon begins with the acceptance of your first registration. From here on, everything starts rolling. Once the date is set, it starts. In this chapter the three phases of the hackathon (start, work, and finish) are discussed in detail. All relevant tasks in the respective phases are described.

Once the preparations for a hackathon are completed, one can look forward to the operation. By the hackathon event itself we mean the period from the first contact with the participants on site until the end of the event. After the operation and the end of the hackathon event the follow-up of the results follows (see Chap. 4). In the following, the aspects that are directly concerned with the implementation of the event are considered. During this entire time the organizers are in contact with the participants. People will meet for the first time, friendships will develop, problems will arise and will be solved. In the end there will be great joy but also disappointments here and there. During the whole time of the event there will be an intensive contact with other people. The organizer is responsible for being a good host during this time. No matter how well prepared the event is, challenges will arise that could not have been foreseen. Improvisation during a hackathon is therefore not a rarity, but rather the rule. The staff on the side of the organizer should therefore be large enough to be able to handle even dicey situations during the whole period of the event.

The individual activities of the preparation are shown graphically in Fig. 3.1.

From now on, the following applies: Whereas previously there was time to think, from now on everything will be done with an eye on the clock. Apart from that, the following also applies: If the preparation phase was conscientiously thought through and the planning points were worked through, there will be very few problems during the operation.

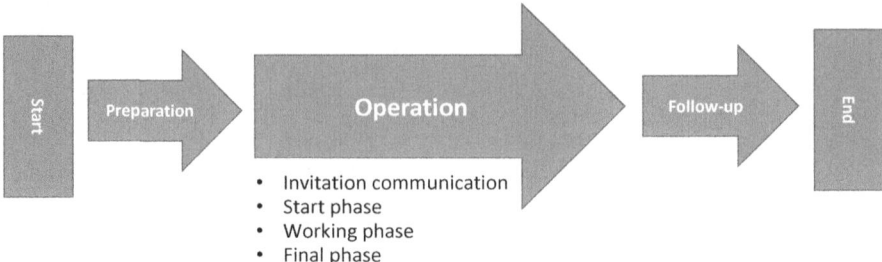

Fig. 3.1 Overview of the individual activities during the implementation

3.1   Invitation Communication

The invitation process has already been addressed under the legal aspects in Sect. 2.3.2. But since it is the first contact to the hackathon participant, which provides him with information and finally leads to registration and his participation, it is important here again. The tasks in the invitation process that need to be provided may not be very specific. But the potential participants who are invited to participate are not the usual visitors of events. The event format also raises more questions than normal and the effort for consultation is considerably higher. Of course, the invitation communication also includes receiving the feedback, managing the registrations, and transmitting the rules for participation. Participation is confirmed by e-mail or letter. It is monitored that the maximum number of participants is not exceeded. Questions should always be answered promptly. The time of invitation communication is the right time for the organizer to get to know the potential participants better:

- Is the participant an individual or part of a team?
- Is it a student, professional, "nerd," founder, or otherwise?
- Is there any interest in venture capital, an internship, or further cooperation?
- What kind of care will the participant need and what skills does he/she bring with him/her?
- From where does he travel, does he stay at the location for the hackathon or externally?
- Is he interested in specific areas of focus?
- Does he have any other wishes or questions?

In a hackathon, each participant requires more attention than in other formats. This increased attention is preceded by the participant's prior consent to the use of the data provided for this purpose. When participating in a hackathon, the participant may incur high travel expenses, spend a lot of time, and may become an important partner for the organizer. It is therefore virtually obligatory to show the participant high esteem for him or her already upon arrival.

3.2 Start Phase

The start phase is very important. It is responsible for the basic mood, the communication of the topics, the introduction of the participants, and the group formation. "There is no second chance for a first impression." This also applies to hackathons. So make sure right from the start that you welcome your participants (but of course also your team and other supporters such as the sponsors) appropriately, provide them with all the necessary information, and make sure that everything feels good right from the start.

The individual points of the first phase are described in detail below.

3.2.1 Before Arrival

The preparation of the rooms and adjoining rooms with regard to complete and identical equipment can be organized shortly before the hackathon. The light conditions, temperature, cleaning condition should be checked. In case of doubt, provide for zones in which these subjectively felt components are different and thus everyone can develop a feeling of well-being. Place cards for the teams and name badges are an advantage. The participants often have different travel times. One should allow the participants very flexible arrival times. On arrival, each participant should be given maximum orientation and a feeling of well-being immediately. The time before the hackathon should be used to get to know each other. Those who like should be allowed to rest and perhaps be able to use retreat possibilities. Possibilities to get drinks or snacks should be pointed out.

Already at this point it becomes clear: This is not a mass event. A hackathon relies on an adequate and coordinated cooperation. One works together as partners from the beginning.

It is desirable to provide the arriving participants with a contact person right at the beginning. A participant can turn to this contact person, he will be helped or at least get a tip to answer his questions.

This service can also be provided by a special app in technology-related hackathons. The arriving participant can scan a Smart Tag or QR-Code via app, is individually greeted by his app, receives important information via a central WhatsApp group or a comparable chat, and receives help if necessary. However, this form of participant support requires a great deal of preparation and is more likely to be implemented in larger digital and IT-related hackathons.

Networking and getting to know each other among the participants should be encouraged, as this not only creates a good working atmosphere, but also enables later synergy effects. There are no limits to the possibilities. For example, certain areas of interest can be placed under the name badges or participants can write keywords on moderation cards and pin them on community boards provided for this purpose.

The most important answers to obvious questions should be revealed without any demand. In addition to the signs directing to the restrooms, the WLAN password is very important. Most of the time, participants have forgotten their pen and pad and this working material should be freely available. A clear announcement about who among the organizers can provide which information saves "asking around." At this point it should also be noted that in IT and digitization-related hackathons many individuals need a small push.

It is important not to burden the start and work phase of the hackathon with the clarification of unclear questions. A test of the organizer can be to put himself temporarily in the position of the participant. If a few people do this at the same time, situations and questions should be foreseeable. Answer any questions that arise beforehand in a welcome paper. Keep the participants reading this paper at the beginning. Important things and information should be repeated. Clarify and explain among other things (in written and/or digital form):

- Where are which rooms (plenum, workrooms, break rooms, WC, sleeping rooms, etc.) located?
- Where can questions be clarified at any time, who is the contact person, and how can they be reached?
- How is the time schedule planned?
- Where and in what form is technical support available?
- Where and in what form is catering provided?
- Which aids are allowed/which are provided?
- What is not allowed and what consequences can be expected?
- What (digital or analog) possibilities for exchange between the participants are offered?
- Who are the sponsors and where can they be reached?
- What are the prizes?
- Who sits on the jury and according to which criteria are the results evaluated?
- How is intellectual property handled?
- Are image and voice recordings made and if so, how are they handled?

3.2.2   What to Bring?

Since not every participant is a hackathon professional, it should be known what every participant has to bring with him. If rental notebooks are provided, you can leave your own device at home. Nobody should have to bring food and drinks. This also applies to pens and pads. However, everyone should be allowed to bring their own pillow for a nap. The invitation communication (see Sect. 2.3.2) should have informed in advance what is provided by the organizer and what participants have to bring.

3.2.3   The Preliminary Program

The pre-program should not be an accumulation of general information, but rather a motivational boost. The beginning of the event determines the speed and verve of the hackathon. Inspiration comes before information. Therefore the choice of speakers should be made with care. Choose a speaker who on the one hand can say something about the given topic in terms of content and on the other hand can carry you away. For larger hackathons, this could be a developer, speaker, or company representative who is well known in the hackathon scene.

The important information (e.g. about the course of events, location, services offered, emergency center, etc.), rules of conduct, and assistance require repetition. These therefore belong in the pre-program and should be announced briefly and memorably.

3.2.4   Organizational Rules and Procedure

Rarely have all participants studied all available information and rarely have the organizers communicated all information in advance. The most important information should therefore be mentioned again in the closing minutes of the pre-program. The possibility to contact someone at the "service desk" at any time is important to mention here.

The fact that in the course of the hackathon everyone is allowed to address each other by the first name can certainly be encouraged. But also the question if teams are allowed to or should interact can be discussed. Cooperation can be stimulated. If many of the participants come from a student environment, the atmosphere will be relaxed. If the participants are rather professionally experienced people, it might be better to work towards a relaxed atmosphere. Here, the (even if only temporary) "familiarity" can break the first ice. The explanation of the seriousness of the hackathon goals does not contradict the statement that a hackathon should also be fun.

After the pre-program, questions about the organization should not occur frequently. Therefore basic rules must have been clarified here. Communicate, for example, the following:

- Room allocations serve the basic organization.
- Smoking regulations are essential.
- Volume discipline is more than just a courtesy call.
- Reference to "cheating."

3.2.5 Showing the Possibilities of Idea Generation

It is due to the nature of the hackathon that the first minutes and perhaps hours will be used for generating ideas. Not everyone is familiar with creativity techniques. But they can be extremely helpful in a team. In the preliminary program, classical techniques such as Method635, Morphological Matrix, and Osbourne Checklist can be mentioned. The participants not only learn more, but also have the chance to develop a well-ordered cooperation in newly composed teams using a fixed method-ology. More detailed literature can be found under "practice-oriented innovation and product management."

3.2.6 Questionnaires

In the first quarter of the event, three-quarters of the questions appear. During this time, several contact persons need to be available. During the hackathon working time, time is the second scarcest commodity behind a great idea. It must be ensured that contact persons for questions are known, but also that special questions can be quickly forwarded to the right people. It must also be clear that participants are themselves responsible for a large number of questions. The organizer should only help where he is responsible. Information beyond that carries the risk of distorting the competition. In technical questions, only one corridor of possible consideration may be shown at any one time; solutions are distortions of competition.

It is best to assign fixed persons for this. Provide (technical) coaches who can help with the local technology, on the one hand, and who can also provide support with regard to possible infrastructures or programming languages for implementation without working on content. Continue to provide personnel who are available to answer other questions. These can be questions about the process, catering, or the organization of breaks. Make sure that the persons are clearly named and introduced at the beginning and are available during the whole time.

3.2.7 Role Allocation

The teams may be advised to divide themselves into roles within their group. For example, it has proven to be a good idea to appoint a team member for quality assurance. Someone who questions the idea and thus provides self-critical advice is just as valuable as someone who is able to defend an idea against criticism. A team leader should not be encouraged, as this hinders the group dynamics. The important role of the time manager should be encouraged. All this is useful to avoid hours of confusion.

For more information on this topic, see also Sect. 5.2.

3.2.8   Prizes

It must be clearly recognizable which prizes are awarded to the hackathon winners. It is even more important that the jury's evaluation criteria are known to all participants beforehand, and that these criteria are applied decisively in the end. If special prizes are awarded, it must be explained in detail how they are to be won.. The evaluation criteria themselves must be presented as well as the proportional weighting of the various evaluation criteria. It should be communicated in advance that the prizes do not represent the sole appreciation. A good hackathon knows no losers and this positive spirit must be communicated very early and again and again.

3.2.9   Motto

The motto of the hackathon with a detailed task description cannot be repeated often enough. Nothing is worse than a motivated team working many hours on the wrong topic. Every participant will try to follow the motto and other guidelines of the hackathon. If time allows, you can also insert an interim presentation for this purpose after half of the implementation time. Here you can see what the individual teams want to implement. If a team is going in the wrong direction you can still intervene here. In addition, you should ask the individual groups at regular intervals about their ideas and the respective implementation status. Here, possible problems and misguided ideas become quickly apparent. If it is possible for the organizer, the repeated explanation of the goal should be part of the keynote.

An important element is the refinement of the hackathon task. In the run-up to the event, initial information on the hackathon task was provided. However, since teams must not be able to prepare themselves completely in advance, the task must be refined in the final minutes. Only if the actual task gets a specialization at the end, there is a real challenge to face this task with creative efforts.

3.2.10 Panel at the Beginning

A panel in the form of selected podium participants, who talk on stage about the given topic or a technology to be used, can enrich the event with many opinions and perspectives. However, a panel is always quite time-consuming. A panel can be a strong entry point if the messages are short and crisp. Furthermore, a panel with well-known personalities can be a real motivator. Moderation of the panel is indispensable, otherwise times will not be kept.

3.2.11 Keynote

A keynote at the beginning decides whether the event is important or rather a conventional event. Who is the right person for goose bumps, appreciation, and represents role model? Whether a board member or an inspiring CIO is basically not important—the right effect must be created. For in-house hackathons, at least the IT manager, if not someone from the management, should give the presentation. At external hackathons, industry leaders or particularly good and well-known speakers (for example, known from sports, radio, or television) are often chosen. The keynote should boost the motivation of the participants at the end of the starting phase and should be the starting signal for the working phase.

3.3   Work Phase

While in the starting phase the participants were condemned to passivity and the organizers had to be very active, the switch is flipped with the beginning of the working phase. The teams know what to do, the organizers switch to a reactive mode and become observers and companions. While the organizer team can rest for a while, the participants are now challenged. Now the mentors and coaches can start their work.

3.3.1   Flyingstart

The transition from the pre-program to the actual work part can be designed as a flying start. The pre-program ends with high condensation of what has been said before, and the work phase begins. This transition can begin, for example, with the presentation of implementation ideas on stage by previously selected participants. In this way the remaining participants can decide on an idea and thus on a possible team. If no concrete ideas have been developed in advance, an open or moderated topic development can be directly connected to the keynote. Thus, the two parts merge seamlessly. This is very good for the participants, as the momentum and motivation from the speeches can be transferred directly into the implementation phase.

3.3.2   Creative Phase

The longest time of a hackathon is the working phase with the respective stages of evolution from the idea to the result. It is often a long way until the final idea is found. Teams that have already worked in advance are always at an advantage here. Teams that have not worked together in advance enjoy the advantage of impartiality and are better able to incorporate the latest information. The design of the work phase is completely left to the teams themselves. Coaching is, if desired, always conceivable. Coaching should refer to methods (for example, creative techniques) or technologies (for example, IT architecture or programming concepts) and should not interfere with the actual creative process with external ideas. In this way, advice on timing can also be given. The creative phase is initially characterized by a lively discourse. In the best case, basis-democratic decision-making processes in the team lead to a result that determines what the next few hours are to be worked on. Flipcharts or blackboards are needed in this phase and should be available to every team. When the creative phase comes to an end, the teams are noticeably calmer from the outside. Teams that get bogged down for too long in an idea-finding phase can be helped.

3.3.3   Implementation

The central part of a hackathon event, after the phase of idea generation and description, is the (at least partial) implementation of the idea. It is important to avoid teams getting bogged down in the implementation process, deviating from the original concept, and ending up without a result. A consistent conceptual design, a well-thought-out idea, and a half-finished work result are at least a partial success. A dissatisfied team that has lost itself in the small details of implementation and then failed will be immensely disappointed. In other words: In a hackathon, you have to plan more roughly and a detailed implementation is out of place if you get stuck in the middle of the implementation. A "fake" does it then. In this phase you can again support with targeted coaching offers. The actual implementation is of course left to the teams.

3.3.4   Part of the Organizer in the Work Phase

The work phase is the longest phase in the hackathon and is, however, subject to the least influence of the organizer. Therefore you have no further tasks here, except to make sure that all accompanying processes (service desk, catering, accommodation, and so on) work smoothly. Persons from the environment of the organizer must always behave neutrally. Sympathies must not lead to unauthorized tips being given. Coaches or other employees of the organizer may not be tempted to actively participate in teams.

Interventions by the organizer may, however, be appropriate if

- a fight breaks out within a team or between teams.
- the brainstorming phase exceeds a quarter of the hackathon working time.
- different teams are going down exactly the same road.
- participants cheat or steal ideas.

3.3.5   Jury Involvement

In order that the jury can make a fair judgment in the end and understand all necessary connections, it should be allowed to have discussions with the teams as a member of the jury. This should not be a constraint or a loss of working time for the teams. Moreover, jury members should only listen and under no circumstances give advice. This procedure should take into account that only communication with all teams means equal opportunities. Any sympathies for teams or individuals should also be noticed and then consciously ignored. Time is now the scarcest good—the organizer and the jury have to keep to this.

3.3.6   Feedback Sheet

The organizer should have distributed a feedback sheet within the working phase at the latest, in which the teams can give their suggestions and feedback. In addition to questions about general satisfaction, questions about premises, catering, and organization may also be asked. In this phase the participants have the most time and the chance of receiving a completed feedback form is high.

3.3.7   Presentation Preparation

An experienced hackathon team will very early on prepare the presentation of their results. A conclusive presentation, good argumentation, and self-confidence in their appearance can make even mediocre performances look outstanding. In addition, experienced presenters are always at an advantage and achieve sympathy points. Inexperienced teams may be helped here, as long as the performance itself is not influenced. All teams need help with time management. The preparation time of the presentation is almost always underestimated. Ten percent of the working time should be suggested as a minimum preparation time. In addition to effective time management, it may also be suggested that the presentation preparation should be parallel from the first minute.

The jury would be well advised to ask the teams about their ideas and implementation plan during the hackathon. This is the only way to enable a speedy jury evaluation later on.

Optionally, intermediate presentations can also be used. However, this possibility must then be equally available to all teams. Should teams wish to present their ideas and results during working hours, this can be allowed. However, this should then be announced in advance as an option. Furthermore, it must not disturb other teams and it must not completely tie up the capacities of the organizer. Assistance from the organizer may not distort competition after the interim presentation.

3.3.8 Presentation Mix

Not every participant knows the different possibilities to present work results successfully. The use of slides is usually the way to go. Videos and graphics can also be used or prototypes can be presented live on stage. Various presenters during the performance should also be encouraged. Here the coaches can again assist in the preparation of the final presentation and give suggestions for a successful presentation.

Make sure that the teams have all technical and other possibilities for the presentation at their disposal and that they work flawlessly. A flickering picture, a too low volume of microphones or music, and unfavorable lighting conditions can spoil the best presentation.

3.3.9 Final Checks

The organizer should carry out a technical check 1 h before the final phase. Meanwhile, a microphone that was still charged 20 h ago may be empty. An adapter that was there 2 h ago may have disappeared. It is always advisable to shift organizational issues onto several shoulders. Improvisation will be part of the final phase of a hackathon, but a professional end of the hackathon gives a good overall impression.

3.3.10 Time Management

When the efforts of the participants slowly come to an end, the final phase becomes even more challenging for the jury and the organizer. The moderator should always point out the remaining time, especially in the hour before the end of the working hours, by appropriate announcements. The teams are then engrossed in their work. The organizer must therefore make himself clearly noticeable. A small bell or an audible signal tone is helpful here. During the last hour, the activity increases significantly—in some places hecticness can break out.

Expect an increasing number of inquiries in the final phase. Most of these will relate to the presentation and the jury. Make sure that you provide all teams with the same information and do not give any team an advantage.

3.3.11 Countdown

The end of the event should be announced 30 min before the end and should be counted down audibly at shorter intervals with a time announcement. For the last 5 min, the teams need to sharpen the announcement to hear the end of the working time. Since this is not a 100-m run, one may also be lenient and add a few seconds or minutes.

3.4   Final Phase

The shortest phase in the hackathon is the final phase. At the same time it decides on winners and non-winners and is therefore also the most emotional and most important phase for the organizer.

The end must be announced very loudly—several times. A horn, a bell, or a microphone is indispensable here. The participants take a deep breath, the organizers get back to work.

The time after the official end of work is to be used extremely efficiently, as by this time everyone present is exhausted and already impatient.

A good hackathon event can use the following guidelines for time management in the final phase (see Table 3.1).

3.4.1   Presentation of Results

The most exciting time has come when the working time is over and the participants have to stop working. One after the other the teams will then present their results to the jury and the other teams.

The presentations should not be shorter than 5 min. Less time reduces the possibility of really addressing all the points of a well-thought-out idea. More than 10 min will lead to too much detail. In such a case the jury is flooded with information. The quality of the presentations held will vary greatly depending on the seniority and life experience of the participants. In hackathon events, however, the focus should be on the achievement of conceiving and implementing a well-thought-out and new idea. Less familiar presenters may therefore be given leniency if a presentation is presented in a somewhat bumpy and uncertain manner. If the actual idea is noteworthy on its merits, this should be given a higher priority than a good presentation. The presentation framework and the presentation medium are usually left to the team. Fairness in the evaluation is only given if strict adherence to the presentation guidelines, especially adherence to the presentation time, is taken into account. The moderator of the event is therefore in demand.

Table 3.1 Timetable of the final phase

What	Who	Duration
Notice of timing	Presenter	3 min
Announce next steps	Moderator	2 min
Presentations	Participants	5–10 min per team
Consultation of the jury	Jury	15 min
Award ceremony	Jury and presenter	15 min
Moderator	Presenter	5 min

3.4.2   Jury Phase and Award Ceremony

The jury should be well organized and come to a conclusion quickly. Prefabricated evaluation forms are ideal for this. The evaluation criteria should also be discussed with a proportional assessment of the fulfillment per team. Despite the short time available, attention should be paid to each team and each idea. A few words of praise should also be pre-formulated for each team.

The jury will make it exciting when all the jurors take over the announcement and use the tension when awarding prizes from back to front to the first places. Each team should be appreciated and the positive results of each team should be mentioned. The spirit of a hackathon, that everyone becomes a winner by participating, should be communicated to the non-winning teams with sensitive words.

How the winning teams are rewarded and what term for the 1st/2rd place is chosen are up to each organizer and may be fun for everyone. For example, platinum, gold, and silver or top performer, winner, or idea hero.

The reasons for the evaluations and ultimately the choice of the winning teams should be very sound and should be based exactly on the criteria named before the start of the hackathon. The jury will hand over certificates and if possible also the prizes. The partners can also support this if they have brought in the corresponding prizes.

The winning teams will be happy, break out in jubilation and these minutes should be captured in a photo documentary. After the hackathon these pictures are the best medium to promote further events of this kind.

3.4.3   Final

Like after sports, it takes time to "calm down." Before the official end is announced, there should be time to rejoice, mourn, and take a breath. In this phase you should give the teams time to exchange ideas internally and discuss the jury's assessments. You should also encourage the exchange between the teams. In this way you can learn something from the respective approaches.

Depending on the size and orientation of the event, investor meetings can also be held and press appointments made. This must be scheduled accordingly and appropriate rooms must be provided.

It is possible that in this phase positive and negative emotions are very high. Make sure that cheering and grief remain fair. Your coaches can become very important in this phase and provide mental support.

3.4.4 Farewell

While the winners will be photographed once more, disappointed candidates may disappear without saying a goodbye. Announce in time that contact will be kept and do not forget to confirm the thanks for participation via e-mail a few days later.

Finally, the individual phases of the implementation are graphically summarized again in Fig. 3.2.

Fig. 3.2 The phases of operation with corresponding roles, actions, and emotions

3.5   Summary

- The starting phase should be used efficiently and should inform and motivate the participants.
- The work phase essentially demands the organizer to be a good host.
- The final phase remains in the minds of organizers and participants for a long time—preferably positive.
- The appreciation in the direction of the teams must be felt at all times.
- The jury must be well-prepared and make a quick and fair decision.
- A good hackathon knows no losers, only winners.
- The goodbye is a calling card for the next hackathon.

Follow-Up

4

Abstract

After a successful planning and operation there must always be a follow-up of the hackathon. This is the only way to ensure that the hackathon can unfold its full power. Unfortunately this part is often neglected or even completely forgotten. So it should be clear to everyone that in the short time of a hackathon most ideas could only be sketched and implemented in the form of prototypes. To push the ideas further or even to found new companies, further time and help is needed in many places. Furthermore (as with any event) a feedback or "lessons learned" round should be held with all team members of the organizer. Also a suitable reporting by the organizer should take place afterwards, to present the results of the hackathon and possibly announce the next one already. In the following the most important activities after a hackathon are presented.

The hackathon is over and the stress level is slowly decreasing for everyone. But only the actual event is over. The hackathon goes even further for the organizers. After a successful planning and operation there always has to be a follow-up of the event. This is the only way to ensure that the hackathon can unfold its full power.

Unfortunately, this part is often neglected or even completely forgotten. This is a pity because there is still a lot to do. So it should be clear to everyone that in the short time of a hackathon most ideas could only be sketched and implemented in the form of prototypes. To push the ideas further or even to found new companies, further time and help is needed in many places. Furthermore (as with any event) a feedback or "lessons learned" round should be held with all team members of the organizer. This ensures that experiences and opinions (of the participants and the team) help to make the next event even better. Also, the organizer should provide a suitable report afterwards to present the results of the hackathon and probably announce the next one already. In the following chapters the most important activities after a hackathon are presented.

The single activities of the follow-up are shown graphically in Fig. 4.1.

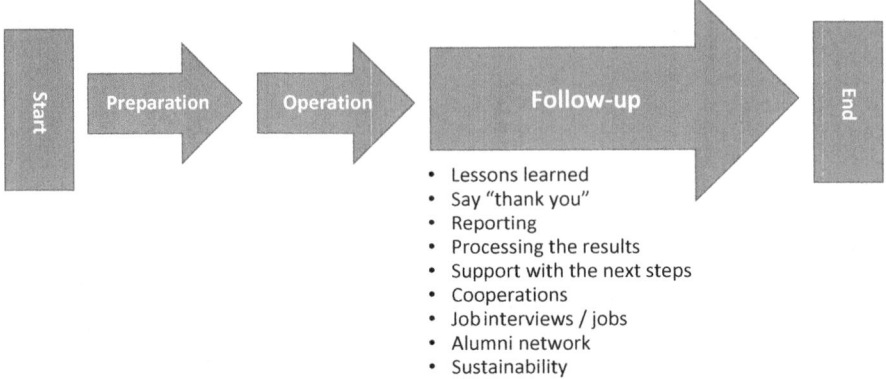

Fig. 4.1 Overview of the individual activities during the follow-up

4.1   Lessons Learned

After the hackathon is over and all participants have left, you should (after the cleanup) take some time with your team. No matter how well you have planned the hackathon, not everything will run smoothly in a hackathon. This makes it all the more important to preserve what has been achieved and to notice mistakes in order to avoid them next time. In the aftermath of the hackathon, all team members involved should therefore be asked to give a short oral or written feedback of their past impressions, on the part of the organizer. This will give you a good insight into what happened "before and behind the scenes" during the event. Use this "maneuver critique" to find out if everything really worked as planned and where there were deviations. Do not evaluate the statements in the first step, but collect everything first. In the next step you can then draw your conclusions.

Continue collecting feedback from participants and sponsors during the event. You can do this by conducting a short survey (digital or paper) towards the end of the event. This will provide you with direct feedback. You should take this feedback seriously and use it when planning future hackathons.

It should also be investigated promptly whether the presumed expenditure of money and personnel was realistically estimated. Even if hackathons as such usually have no profit intentions, they should at least be fully paid for with the help of the collected sponsor money and other revenues. Therefore the financial evaluation of the event is an important action. Check how much money you have raised in advance (e.g. through sponsors) and during the event (e.g. through the sale of drinks and food) and hold your expenses against it. At best, there will be some money left over after the event, which can then be invested in communication activities. Otherwise, there should be a "black zero" under the bottom line. Otherwise, you need to see how you deal with the loss. It is possible that one of the sponsors will step in afterwards. In any case, use this calculation to better estimate the income and costs for your next hackathon. This will make financial planning for the next event easier right from the start.

Continue to evaluate all available metrics that are available to you. Note that it is best to determine what metrics you want to measure, how you want to measure them, and how you define a successful event right in the planning stage. Some values can be collected by simple counting, some can be asked, and others can only be perceived by feeling. Possible criteria would be, for example:

- The reach of the advertising campaign in the run-up
- Number of registrations
- Number of registered but not attending participants ("no-show-rate")
- Number of sponsors
- Money raised (through sponsors and other sources)
- Number of teams (+ average number of team members)
- Evaluation of the results
- Number of sponsor meetings
- Number of investor meetings
- Number of jobs or job interviews
- Number of press mentions (in magazines and online)
- Number of likes, (re-)tweets, number of new followers on social media, etc.
- Feedback from participants, sponsors, and team members
- Other feedback (location, security forces, paramedics, residents, etc.)

With all this information you can evaluate the just finished hackathon well and derive possible improvements for a next one. Try to get a little better at every event. You will succeed in doing so simply by following the routine that comes with time. It is best to run a continuous improvement process directly at the first event (see [7]). This will help you to improve with each pass. The classical process (also called PDCA (Plan, Do, Check, Act) or Deming cycle) consists of four parts (see Fig. 4.2):

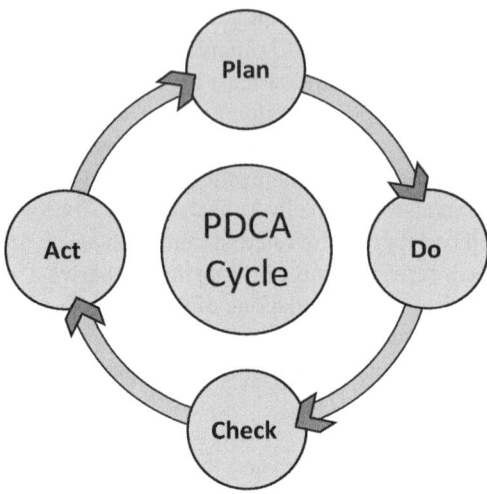

Fig. 4.2 The PDCA cycle (cf. [7])

1. *Plan:* Here (as described in Chap. 2) the hackathon is planned with all its aspects. Also define your (measurable) success criteria here.
2. *Do:* In the next step the actual event is held. Important metrics and opinions are already collected in order to be able to check them in the next step.
3. *Check:* After the hackathon, conduct a feedback and "lessons learned" round as described in this chapter and compare your plan and goals with the hackathon results and data collected.
4. *Act:* In the last step you draw your conclusions from the results of the previous step and use the knowledge to improve the next hackathon.

After you have evaluated the hackathon in every respect, as described in this chapter, and have drawn your conclusions, you can start planning your next hackathon, true to the motto: "After the hackathon is before the hackathon!".

4.2   Thank You

The work of the team members, the involvement of the sponsors, and of course the commitment of the participants are on a voluntary basis. Without all these people a hackathon could not take place. So after the hackathon it is time to say "thank you". Nowadays the best way to reach all participants is by mail. So set up an appropriate mail for each target group (if possible within 1 week after the event). The mail should contain the thank you, a feedback from you, a short summary of the event, and a short description of the winners and their ideas. Furthermore, you should include photos of the event or link to your homepage in order not to make the attachment too large. Furthermore you can also refer to video material or a video summary on your site or on a video portal of your choice. You can also add a small press review with the most important reports and posts from the internet.

In addition to this general information, you should provide concrete data to the sponsors and other financial backers. This can be (if appropriately anchored in the terms and conditions), for example, data on the number of participants, the "no-show-rate," or even entire participant lists. At the same time, you can also provide photos of the advertising inventory, the posters hung up, the flyers laid out, or roll-ups set up as proof. If your planning for another hackathon has already begun, you can use the communication directly to win possible sponsors for the upcoming event.

As already mentioned, you should of course also thank your team separately. This should be done (in addition to the thanks at the end of the hackathon) in a more personal mail. Here you can thank them again especially for their dedication and commitment. Maybe you tell a few anecdotes from the planning and/or operation or include small memories of the participants. You should also include a group photo of all helpers, which you can take at the end of the event. This way you show your appreciation and at the same time motivate them to participate again.

Use any thank you e-mails to collect further feedback. Positive feedback can be a balm for the soul after a stressful event. Negative feedback should be used as a suggestion for improvement. It is best to refer to a short, online-based questionnaire for the survey. You can find appropriate tools by a specific search on the internet. Many of the tools are even free of charge and are perfectly adequate for this purpose. Prepare different questionnaires for participants, sponsors, and backers as well as your team. Offer yes/no questions, questions with a rating scale (for example, between 1 and 10, school grades, or "I fully agree" to "I do not agree at all"), and questions with free text answers. Possible questions for the participants could be:

- How satisfied were you overall with the hackathon?
- How satisfied were you with the preparation?
- Was the communication in advance sufficient?
- How can we improve the preparation for the next time?

You will find further questions for your feedback forms in the checklists in Chap. 10.

4.3 Reporting

Hackathons are often picked up by the media. Try to get (local) newspapers or industry media interested in a report. Media partnerships can also be established for this purpose. For example, reporters can take photos and record interviews at the event and then write an article. You may even be able to integrate (local) television. But this depends entirely on the size, an outstanding topic, or the outcome of the hackathon.

Furthermore, you should already have reports online during the hackathon. For larger hackathons, it is worth assigning a separate role in your team whose task (among other things or even exclusively) is digital communication. For example, set up a Twitter, Facebook, and/or Instagram account with corresponding hashtags for communication. Additionally, you can upload videos to online platforms such as YouTube or Vimeo. Report from the organizer's point of view, capture participant quotes, and interview the sponsors. This is how you create a "panoramic view." You can also actively use the "like" and forwarding functions of the corresponding platforms and networks to quickly distribute content generated by the participants. In this way, you can show that you are also following the opinions of the participants and easily gain access to additional material for your communication channels. Consolidate all content centrally on your homepage. In this way, you can give all interested parties a quick overview, exchange views, and stay in touch.

Afterwards, write a summary on your homepage and publish pictures of the event and the award ceremony. Share this again via your social networks and offer the report to other online (specialist) sites for distribution. Keep on summarizing the ideas of the teams and report about little stories that happen on the event or behind the scenes of the hackathon. A good follow-up report is also good advertising for the next hackathon.

4.4   Processing the Results

During the hackathon, the teams had little opportunity to get closer to the ideas and work results of the other teams. Mostly only the short impression of the final presentation remains. But in the aftermath, the ideas, products, solutions, business models, and above all their technical implementation can be of great interest to everyone. Therefore, it is a good idea to compile a short, perhaps illustrated, compilation of the entire results. This information can then be made available in the member area of the homepage and included as an addition to the feedback mail.

It makes sense to think about the type and structure of the report in advance. It is best to communicate the structure already at the time of registration so that everyone knows how their results will be made available to others (and possibly also to investors) afterwards. For the presentation of business models the Business Model Canvas has become established in recent years (see [9]). The Canvas allows to display a complete business model with all aspects on one page. Thus, not only the actual core of the business model, but also the costs and revenue sources including marketing are depicted. Figure 4.3 shows the template of the Business Model Canvas. Often this tool is already used by the teams during the hackathons.

Structural graphics of the individual components (for example: web server, database, application server, etc.) and their dependencies have become established for the representation of the technical implementation. For the representation of software structures and processes UML (Unified Modeling Language, see [2]) has established itself as a graphical tool. In addition, you should also include photos of the prototypes. This allows a visual impression. You may also be able to include a video of the corresponding final presentations. This way, all interested parties have a complete overview of all projects.

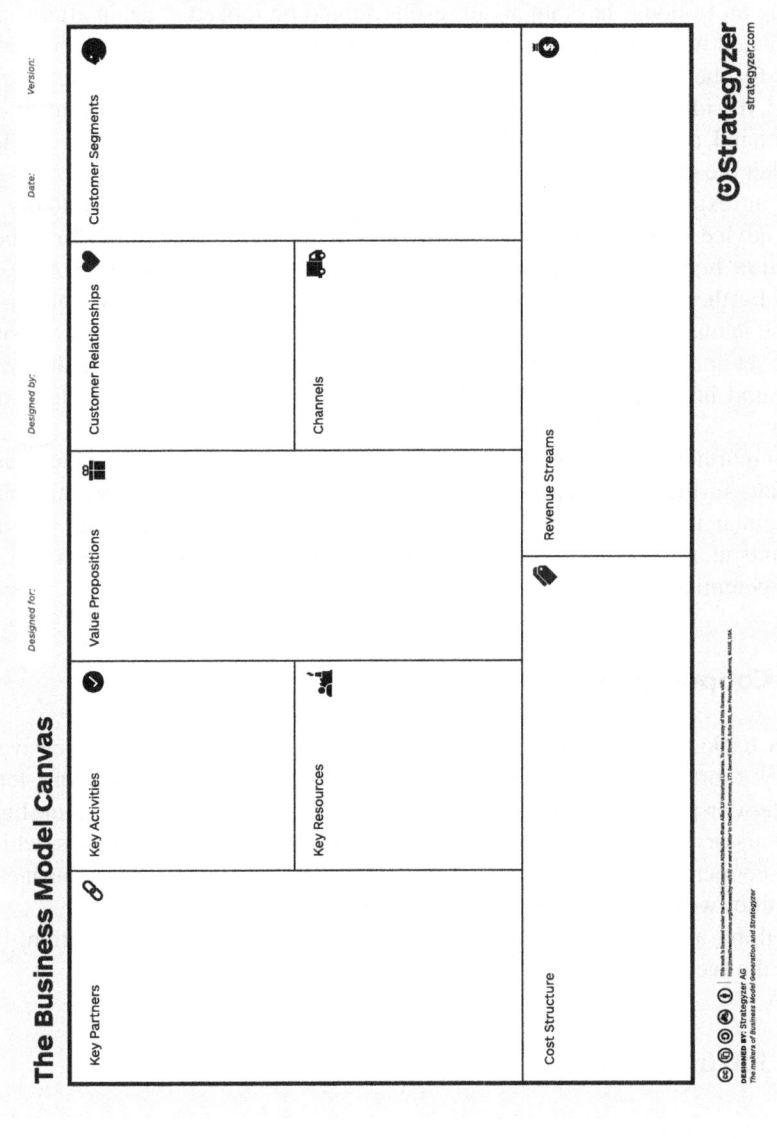

Fig. 4.3 The Business Model Canvas. This graphic is provided by Strategyzer AG under the creative commons license (CC BY-SA 3.0)

4.5   Supporting the Next Steps

During a hackathon, good ideas and their implementation can at best be sketched and presented with the help of a prototype. However, many teams would like to develop their projects further after the event for various reasons.

During an in-house hackathon, all results should be looked at again afterwards and evaluated with regard to their market chances. If at least one idea is considered valuable for the company, it must be determined how this should be done. On the one hand, the idea can be handed over to the in-house development department, on the other hand, a new company (e.g. a "Spin Off") can be founded to further develop and market the idea.

After an external hackathon, you can offer the participants the opportunity to provide advice and support after the event. For example, you can offer expert consultation hours or online forums where participants can get tips on how to proceed. Furthermore, you can also arrange or make available temporary premises where the teams can continue working. If an idea is so good that a new company might be set up, you can also offer support in setting up a new company. In this way, you can find investors, offer legal advice, or give tips on personnel and financial planning.

It is important that you think about how you want to deal with the results and participants in the follow-up before the hackathon. Prepare appropriate material, allocate financial resources and build up an supporting network. Avoid leaving participants alone after the event. This causes displeasure on all sides and wastes possible potential.

4.6   Cooperations

During a hackathon many people and companies work together very intensively in a very short time. It is worthwhile to check afterwards whether long-term cooperation or partnerships can be derived from the initial business relationships. So sponsors or investors and organizers can conclude appropriate contracts, which secure a cooperation for the next hackathons. It is possible that further (business) opportunities will arise from the initial hackathon-related relationships.

Also think about not immediately obvious partnerships with the location, the caterers, the security staff, etc.

4.7   Job Interviews

If you as a company have organized a hackathon, or you have participated as a partner/sponsor in a hackathon to find new employees, now is the time to ask the participants for a written application. If you do not want to do this, or if participants gave you application documents directly at the event (which is not uncommon), you should write to the candidates promptly and invite them for an interview. Whether you are looking for freelancers (i.e. external freelancers for a specific project), permanent employees, or interns is of course up to you. Do not let too much time pass after the hackathon. The candidates looking for a new job have certainly not only talked to you. Sometimes the candidates are so sought after that employment contracts are already offered at the hackathon. In times of shortage of skilled workers this is also not uncommon. Bear in mind that you are in a very fast moving and dynamic industry and that applicants can now freely choose the jobs they want.

4.8 Alumni Network

Although the cooperation in a hackathon was limited in time, it was intensive. Some people will want to keep in touch and may be interested in further exchange afterwards, want to stay informed, or stay connected to the organizer. If you are planning to offer more hackathons in the future, you might want to create an alumni network. In this way, you give participants, investors, sponsors, and other interested parties the opportunity to stay in contact beyond the actual event.

The network can then be used to offer technical forums, for example. Furthermore job exchanges are very popular. Additionally you can advertise your next hackathons and of course you can enable purely interpersonal contact. An alumni network can be set up like a club, send out regular information, and invite to member meetings. A corresponding network can also be set up by setting up a group in a social network or a closed member area on your homepage.

Through regular information relevant to the respective target group (also beyond the topic of hackathons) you offer added value for your alumni in addition to the exchange platform. The aim is to bind the participants to you and to build a loyal and reliable network.

4.9 Sustainability

A date for a second review should be set shortly after the hackathon. After a few months, it is much easier to judge whether the hackathon has produced sustainable results. Also, whether the conceived ideas could be further developed or whether the cooperation with newly met people could be continued only becomes apparent in the follow-up. An assessment of whether the effort expended justified the benefit can also only be made after some time.

This approach applies to publicly organized hackathons as well as to in-house hackathons. With public hackathons it is good to know whether something has developed from the ideas. Maybe one or the other successful company was founded. Maybe ideas were bought up by big companies or investors. Try to keep up with the ideas and the participants through your network. Maybe you will soon be able to advertise your next hackathon with real success stories.

For in-house hackathons, sustainability is even more important because you have invested time and money in the event to develop innovative new business ideas. The ideas developed during the hackathon must now be carefully checked for their marketability afterwards. How you set up this process and who is responsible for it should already be clarified before the hackathon. Otherwise the ideas will fizzle out and the added value will be lost. If you have found an idea that represents real added value for your customers, you must now transfer it to your classic development and develop it into a real product.

If you regularly hold in-house hackathons, you should also closely monitor the development of ideas from previous events in addition to the ideas from the last hackathon. Check whether the ideas really became products that are in demand on the market. You should leave this task to your business development department (for more information on this topic and suggestions on how to set up such a process, see [7]).

4.10 Summary

- After the hackathon, sit down with your team and conduct an open and honest "lessons learned" session. Make use of the feedback from participants, partners, and sponsors. This helps to reflect good and bad and to get better at the next run.
- Afterwards, please thank all the participants, sponsors, investors, and especially your team.
- Report about the event, the results, and the experiences. Use various channels such as social media, print media, and, if possible, radio and television.
- Prepare the results of the individual teams. In this way the ideas can be reproduced by all interested parties.
- Support the teams that show interest in the next steps. No matter if the started project should be developed further for fun or if a new company should be founded.
- Check whether long-term partnerships can be formed from the business relationships with partners, sponsors, and other service providers established before and during the hackathon.
- If you have used the hackathon as a recruiting tool or received applications, you should contact the applicants and interested parties as soon as possible and schedule interviews.
- A good way to stay in contact with all interested parties and offer an exchange platform is to found an alumni network.
- Ensure that the results obtained are developed further with the appropriate relevance in a sustainable manner. This is the only way to really get the most out of the hackathon.

Participant View

5

Abstract

After the steps for a hackathon implementation were described in detail in the previous chapters, this chapter takes the perspective of a participant. We will look at the reasons for participating in a hackathon and what makes the format so fascinating. Afterwards it is described what a participant can do to get the best possible results. Furthermore, the personal preparation for a hackathon is explained. Finally, it is described what a participant should do after a hackathon in order not to lose energy, contacts, and ideas.

So far in this book it was always assumed that you want to organize your own hackathon. This was described in detail in the previous chapters. In the following the perspective of a participant is taken and it is explained why participants are interested in hackathons at all and what makes the fascination of this format. The following describes what you can do to emerge from a hackathon as successful as possible. Furthermore it is described how to prepare for a hackathon in the best possible way and what you should pack in order to survive the stressful and exhausting time as well as possible. Finally, it will be explained what you should do after participating in a hackathon, so that the energy of the event, the newly gained contacts, and the freshly developed ideas are not lost.

A lot goes through the minds of the participants. Some thoughts are shown in Fig. 5.1.

5.1   Reasons for Participation

There are many reasons for participating in a hackathon. These depend not least on personal inclinations. Often there are several reasons that come together as motivation for participation. In the following the most common reasons are listed without claiming to be complete and without prioritizing.

Fig. 5.1 The participants of a hackathon have many ideas in their heads

- *Meet like-minded people:* Hackathons attract tech-savvy people. Everyone brings with them a deep expertise in their own particular field. This makes it easier to exchange ideas on specialist topics such as special hardware, rare programming languages, or the development of new digital business models because hackathons bring together many like-minded people in one place and bring them into a creative exchange. Often technical specialists in particular do not find anyone in their professional or private environment with whom they can exchange ideas on their topics. Hackathons are the ideal place for this.
- *Contacts:* Hackathons are a great way to make new contacts. Which kinds of contacts are sought in particular depends again on the personal goals. It is certainly possible to easily meet and exchange information with new people and possibly stay in touch beyond the event. Often new friendships are made in this

way. Furthermore it is of course possible to contact sponsors and investors to present your own ideas and possibly get support. Furthermore it is possible to search for new employers. It is not uncommon for letters of application to be handed out directly at hackathons or job interviews to be offered immediately.

- *Teamwork experience:* Even if hackathons are now sometimes huge events with hundreds or even over a thousand participants, there is often (especially within the teams) a very collegial, almost familiar atmosphere. All participants of a hackathon are in the broadest sense enthusiastic about technology and bring along a lot of curiosity and fun in the new. This welds them together and often provides a "we-feeling" from the first minute on. The common interests and the goal of having to solve a concrete task together in the shortest possible time bind people closely together (even if only for 48 h). The goal can only be achieved if everyone pulls together and everyone gives their best. This feeling can rarely be conveyed in such intensity in a normal workplace. Therefore many participants come to such events after the first hackathon again and again to experience this feeling again.

- *Search challenges:* Many participants of a hackathon specifically seek the challenge to find a new solution for a given problem within a short period of time and to implement it (at least partially) with a mixed team. The thrill and pressure of the event give many participants the "kick." This, in combination with the opportunity to try out new technologies and to grow together with like-minded people in the challenge, is for many the real goal of a hackathon.

- *New learnings:* With every hackathon there is something new to learn. Be it a new technology, the handling of a new hardware or software, a new programming language or API (Application Programming Interface), or a new soft skill (for example, patience, giving presentations, teamwork, etc.). This and the exchange with like-minded people ensure that every participant in a hackathon always learns something new, even if it is only after a great effort to lose anyway.

- *Self-promotion:* Hackathons these days are flanked by the media on a grand scale. This begins with the announcement and ranges from (online-based) reporting, some of which is even streamed live, to reports in newspapers, news in social media channels like Facebook, Twitter, and television. By participating in a corresponding interview, for example, the level of awareness can be quickly increased. Many participants also report from the first-person perspective and send short videos, text messages, or pictures. Some participants deliberately stage themselves in order to raise their profile in their field of expertise, with potential employers or investors. The successful participation in hackathons has long become a highly regarded award in application documents.

- *Promoting your own ideas:* Especially at the big hackathons, which attract many investors, many young entrepreneurs present their new business ideas to the public for the first time. At the event, it can be tested in the shortest possible time whether the idea is viable and a prototype shows the feasibility. The best ideas are often immediately provided with investor capital and it is not uncommon for a company to be founded directly after a hackathon. This opportunity is of course a big magnet for participants, which constantly ensures high numbers of participants and new ideas.

- **Winning prizes:** In conclusion, it must of course also be mentioned that the prizes that beckon the winners are often very lucrative and are therefore in themselves reason enough for many to participate.

5.2   How Do I Win at a Hackathon?

Admittedly, this headline is somewhat luridly formulated, but winning does not always mean that you will emerge as the winner. Always remember that in every hackathon you can gain a lot of experience, new contacts, and friends. The real goal of any hackathon should be to learn something and try something new.

Of course, there is no secret recipe for winning a hackathon, but there are many factors that can increase your chances of success.

A hackathon is not an individual competition, but a team competition. Therefore, the most important thing is to have the best possible team composition. Choose your team in a way that you can offer the greatest added value in terms of content on the one hand and that you have a great interest in the topic on the other hand. Make your own strengths and weaknesses clear and then try to find people who can contribute additional skills so that weaknesses are balanced out as far as possible. For this purpose it is important to choose a balanced team or to put one together yourself. Make sure that you have good developers in your team. They form the core of each team because in the end it is mostly about creating software. Keep in mind that you need developers with different characteristics. For example, you need developers for the (mostly web-based) frontend, the backend, the actual business logic, interfaces to third-party systems, and specialists for UI/UX.[1] If the hackathons are different (e.g. hardware-based), you might want to include other or additional skills. In addition, you also need other skills. For example, it helps to have a strong business developer in the team who can align the development with market requirements and create and evaluate appropriate business models for the new solution (see [7]). This ensures that a real added value is generated and that the developed solution solves a real problem. This is often a central evaluation criterion for the jury, as potential commercialization is often sought. Additionally, plan a good speaker for your presentations. This is also an important factor since not only the content but very often the presentation itself is included in the final evaluation. Depending on the planned implementation, you may also need a graphic designer who can develop graphics, images, symbols, color concepts, and slide layouts.

In the next step, you should assign fixed roles within the group right at the beginning and define the associated responsibilities and expectations of each other

---

[1] UI stands for "user interface" and represents the graphical interface between the actual program and the user. UX stands for "user experience." This refers to the usability of a software. A software should be intuitive to use and in the best case even barrier-free.

and communicate them clearly. Make sure that you have realistic expectations of your team members. Keep in mind that everyone works differently: Some work faster, some slower, some need pressure, and still others want to work on their own after an agreement. Additionally, if necessary, appoint a group leader and discuss how to decide in cases of conflict or disagreement.

Also decide at the beginning with which development model you want to work. Mostly agile development is used (often with Scrum[2]). Establish regular coordination and exchange rounds in which everyone must participate. In this way you ensure optimal coordination within the team, keep everyone informed, and can flexibly determine the further course of action. Do not set yourself unrealistic goals. Divide the tasks at hand into packages as small as possible, which can then be processed in between the coordination meetings. In this way you can readjust again and again and do not get lost. There is no time for that during a hackathon.

In the first step, after the actual task is clearly defined, collect implementation ideas and plans. Then choose the best solution for you in the group and prioritize the resulting subtasks accordingly. Additionally, define the critical path of the project. This is the set of tasks that are absolutely necessary to achieve your goal. These tasks must be completed in the correct sequence and in the best possible way. These tasks have top priority. In everything you do, keep in mind that you have a fixed time limit that you must meet. Anything that you do not complete in this time cannot be evaluated. Therefore, a very important task is to estimate the duration of the individual tasks as accurately as possible and to monitor the time required to complete them closely and adjust them if necessary. Do not overestimate what you can achieve in the given time.

To speed up the development processes and to ensure a regular exchange of the created source code, you should always use a program for software version control (e.g. GIT or SVC). These solutions allow several developers to work together on the same files, save the intermediate states, and allow for versioning and time-controlled rollbacks in case of errors. Further define the so-called Writing Conventions. These are rules that clearly tell developers how to structure the source code, how to define variables, and how to comment on the code. This makes collaboration easier, as the readability of the program code is significantly increased and work is done according to uniform conventions.

Make sure that you create a prototype early on. This may already be a digital prototype (for example, using wireframes[3]). Or you can first create an analog

---

[2]Scrum is an agile process model that is often used to create software. The implementation of the software is broken down into small manageable sub-goals which are then worked through step by step. The intermediate goals can be adapted dynamically during development. This provides great flexibility (see [10]).

[3]Wireframes are graphical representations of a program or web application that do not yet have any program logic. However, they provide an impression of the later product early on in the project and allow the discussion of different application scenarios.

prototype (for example, a paper prototype[4]). If the hackathon is not intended to develop software but hardware or a tangible object or product, you should also create a prototype early on. This prototype does not have to consist of the final materials, but can consist of paper, plasticine, Lego bricks, other materials, or a combination of several materials. Using the prototype, you can check various product features at an early stage and discuss them with other participants using a real artifact and collect opinions on how to improve them. This in turn accelerates the development process as a whole, since possible design errors are detected early on and do not have to be eliminated later at great expense. In addition, the prototypes can already be used in possible interim presentations to the jury, as the final product is not yet presentable at this stage.

During the actual development, follow the motto "Reuse everything!". This means that you can assume that when you are dealing with concrete programming tasks and the problems that come with them, many programmers before you have had the same (or a similar) problem. Often the solutions are then even published on the internet as source code, finished programs, interfaces, scripts, or APIs for free use. So you can reuse a lot. Of course this saves a lot of time and speeds up the development process.

When planning and creating your presentation to the jury, make sure that you tell a good story, which in the best case is underlaid with suitable media (slides, videos, music, pictures, etc.). Build up a comprehensible tension and spice up (if possible and appropriate) the presentation with a small (personal) anecdote or joke. Please note, however, that there is usually a time limit for the presentations as well, which you must adhere to. Practice the presentation in advance, collect feedback, and work on a trenchant presentation that describes your problem, your solution, and the added value to the point. When planning your presentation, also consider who is on the jury and what the individual jurors place the greatest value on. Check where the jury members come from, in which environment they work, and find out what criteria they have used in previous hackathons. Adapt your presentation and your statements to the requirements as best as possible. Good presentations "sell" your project and can make the difference in a tight jury decision.

Finally, pay attention to your health. Sleep as much as possible before a hackathon and sleep (if possible) during the hackathon (even if only for a short time). Take a break at least every 2–3 h, eat regularly, and above all drink a lot. Get some fresh air and exercise in between. Do not burden your body with fatty food and do not drink too much caffeine and at best no alcohol. This will ensure that you are physically and mentally fit and can do your best.

But do not forget to have fun with all the suggestions and enjoy the event as a whole with all its aspects. Exchange ideas, talk to many people, and learn from

---

[4]A paper prototype is a one-to-one replica of the later user interface on paper. This is done by using individual pages to indicate different states of the program. Menus are then simulated by placing different pieces of paper on top of each other. In this way, the operation, the visual design, and possible program sequences can be visualized and tested at an early stage.

them. If you keep all this in mind, nothing will stand in the way of success at your next hackathon and the event will be a real win for you, regardless of the final result.

5.3 Personal Preparation

As so often in life, a good preparation also helps with a hackathon. Read the rules and the planned course of the event in good time and think carefully about what you need. This includes not only what items and software you need, but also what features/skills are expected of you and what you can actually contribute. Compare this expectation with yourself and consider if there is anything you can learn in advance that could be useful to you in the hackathon.

If the next hackathon should not be your first one, think about what you can reuse from the previous results. These can be infrastructure plans, process sketches, code snippets, or entire programs. Continue to read up on any given topics. Research the software, hardware, or (web) interface to be used and collect all the information. Store documentation and, if necessary, user manuals on your computer so that you can quickly access them during the hackathon.

Furthermore, you can already create templates for the interim and final presentations, for example, in PowerPoint (or a comparable program). This makes the later process easier because you and your team only have to think about the content.

Install on your computer all tools you plan to use. You may need to install additional software on site, but most of the work can be done in advance and configured so that you can work optimally. This also saves time and leaves you more time to deal with the actual problem.

Additionally, you should set a goal for the hackathon in advance. What do you want to achieve? Certainly not only the victory or place among the top three teams counts. Goals can also be the (professional/technical) exchange with new friends, networking with new people and possible employers or sponsors. Another goal can be to present your own idea and, if necessary, to find investors and co-founders for a new company. Think further about what you can learn or in the broadest sense take away from the hackathon.

Further preparation is certainly possible, but depends on individual preferences and the particular circumstances of the hackathon. Therefore no further concrete tips can be given here.

Finally, an exemplary packing list is presented here, which lists important items that you should take along to a successful hackathon (see Sect. 10.4.3):

- Laptop with appropriate software (development tools, presentation tools, image editing software, etc.)
- Laptop and mobile phone charger (optional: power bank)
- Keyboard and mouse (optional)
- USB stick and/or external hard disk
- Pencil and paper
- Backpack and small carrying bag (for promotional gifts, prices, and brochures)

- Deodorant
- Toothbrush and toothpaste
- Additional change of clothes (pyjamas if desired)
- Towel
- Soap and/or shower gel
- Antibacterial wipes and/or disinfection spray
- Sleeping bag, blanket, and pillow
- Refillable bottle
- Possibly needed medicine
- Earplugs
- Possibly special hardware and tools for hardware hacks
- If desired: music (on mobile phone or other device) and headphones (with noise reduction if possible)
- Optional: books and (card) games for breaks

5.4   And After That?

Chapter 4 described what to consider after the hackathon event. The following is a description of what you can do as a participant after the event to get the best out of it.

After you have recovered from the strains of the hackathon and have had a good night's sleep, you should take some time to review the event. Ask yourself the following questions, for example:

- How did the hackathon go?
- What was good?
- What was not so good?
- How was my time management?
- How did we work together as a team?
- What strengths/weaknesses have I noticed in myself?
- What have I learned?
- Which ideas could I develop further?
- What contacts have I made and how do I use them for my network?
- Was I well prepared?
- What could I learn from this and do better next time?

Be honest with yourself when answering the questions. It will help you to develop yourself further. Use the result to further develop your strengths and to learn from mistakes and misjudgments (for example, in terms of time management, technologies, or people).

In the next step, go through your newly acquired contacts (other participants, sponsors, investors, potential employers, press members, etc.) and connect with them via social or other business networks. Think about what you can do with the new contacts afterwards, how they can help you, and how you can help them. Stay in touch and build up a network that is reliable for all sides. A good network always consists of give and take.

Finally, you should take another close look at the results of your participation. What else can you possibly use from it? Maybe you can use some of the functionalities later on? Maybe you can continue to use whole functions or code blocks of your software? Is the idea or prototype viable? Is it even worthwhile to think about founding your own company? Always consider including the other participants in your group, since the implementation and intellectual property rights are owned by the whole group.

Finally, summarize your results and use them to be better prepared for the next hackathon.

5.5 Summary

- There are many good reasons to participate in a hackathon. These can be, for example, learning new skills, self-marketing, or winning prizes.
- Become aware of your own motivation in advance of a hackathon.
- Prepare for a hackathon as much as possible and plan what you want to achieve.
- A hackathon does not end after the awards ceremony. Make sure that you continue to network afterwards, develop ideas, and take advantage of possible job or business opportunities.

Criticism

6

Abstract

Hackathons are often touted as miracle events where all participants are at their best and find creative solutions to problems in record time. However, there is a serious criticism of the format and the operation. This criticism addresses the way in which commercial success and innovation are to be enforced, sometimes under great pressure to perform.

Since the present book takes a holistic view of the topic of hackathons, the following chapter also introduces the criticism of hackathons and presents possibilities to avoid problems.

Hackathons are often touted in the media as true miracle events where all participants get in top form and find creative solutions to problems in record time. But there is quite serious criticism of the format and the operation. This criticism addresses the way in which commercial success and innovation are to be enforced, sometimes under great pressure to perform. The critique can be divided into two parts: The first part criticizes the format in general and is directed against the format and the operation. However, it turns out that many of the points of criticism raised can be invalidated by good planning and considerate implementation. The second part criticizes especially the internal hackathons. The main argument is that employees are put under pressure in their spare time to develop innovative new product ideas for the company. These points are certainly valid, but they can also be resolved (in part) with appropriate rules.

6.1   General Criticism

Criticism of the format and operation of hackathons has been voiced in various places and by various groups of people. On the one hand there are (justified) complaints from participants or the organizer in the aftermath of hackathons. On the other hand, there is also criticism from sociologists and other scientists who deal with the phenomenon of "hackathons" as a whole.

Hackathons have to accept a lot of criticism regarding the living conditions of the participants during the event. The following points are often criticized:

- **Sleep:** One of the most frequently cited criticisms relates to the lack of sleep during a hackathon. The event usually begins on a Friday afternoon or evening and continues through Sunday. This often means 2 or 3 days of work under high pressure. Many participants do not sleep at all or sleep much too little during this time. This is of course a great strain and at the same time makes the concentration decrease enormously. But even if participants want to sleep, this is only possible if there is enough room for it in the location. In addition, it must be ensured that there is an appropriate noise level in the bedrooms. Many hackathons forget this or do not implement it properly, so that tired participants often cannot get the much needed sleep.

  In order to counteract this, when planning a hackathon you should make sure that the bedrooms are large enough and that they are located as far away as possible from the rooms for group work and lectures. This lowers the volume in the rooms. In addition, you can distribute earplugs and make sure that the bedrooms are kept quiet by appropriate personnel on site.

- **Nutrition:** Another often mentioned point of criticism refers to the nutrition of the participants during a hackathon. In order to stay awake and fit for work for the duration of the event, large amounts of caffeine are often consumed in the form of coffee and highly sugary energy and soft drinks. However, these only suppress the feeling of tiredness for a short time and stimulate the circulation. Long-term consumption can even be harmful to health. Excessive alcohol consumption, however, is less common, as alcohol has a negative effect on concentration and participants often avoid drinking. Furthermore, during a hackathon, people often only eat sporadically and quickly between meals. Fast food is often used, which can be ordered quickly and which satisfies the hunger, but is not good for health in the long run.

  During your hackathons, make sure that the participants drink enough water. You should offer this free of charge. You can also offer tea in sufficient quantities. In this way you provide at least one alternative and a healthy change. You should also make sure that all participants drink enough because a hackathon is very exhausting and the brain needs enough fluid. Also make sure that healthy food is prepared on site and sold at reasonable prices. You can also offer fruit and vegetables locally. In this way you do your best to prevent health problems.

Especially for larger events, make sure that there is sufficient medical first aid on site. In some countries this is even mandatory for events and certain participant sizes and can lead to severe penalties if not observed. Ask the relevant authorities and implement the respective requirements accordingly.

- *Sanitary facilities:* Another often criticized topic is the sanitary facilities. Sometimes these are not designed for large numbers of participants. This can lead to long waiting times. Note especially that in addition to the normal toilet visits, sleep preparation also requires time and space in the bathrooms. You should also ensure that the toilets are cleaned regularly throughout the entire period. Schedule sufficient personnel for this.
- *Psychological pressure:* In addition to the points mentioned so far, the psychological pressure and stress is often criticized which the participants often put on themselves. Many hackathons are about big prize money or even the financial future of young start-ups. This point cannot be invalidated, mitigated, or avoided. At least not at hackathons, which offer monetary or material prizes as a reward besides fun.

  Furthermore, under the stressful conditions of a hackathon, disputes between the individual participants can arise. This can start as a factual/technical argument, go on to insults, and can escalate to physical violence. These cases do not occur too often, but appropriate precautions should be taken. This already starts with the rules of the hackathon. Here you should be open, friendly, and appreciative of each other. Non-observance or gross violations can lead to exclusion in the worst case. From a certain number of participants you should also think about using security personnel.
- *Intellectual property:* The final point of criticism relates to the handling of intellectual property rights of ideas developed during a hackathon. Some hackathons are designed to develop new ideas quickly and turn them into money even faster. The participants are not always involved in the later implementation and in such cases there are often disputes that have to be taken to court because a lot of money can be involved. In such hackathons the later handling of the rights is not clearly regulated in parts and not at all in advance. Therefore the organizers are sometimes even accused of exploitation of the participants.

  Therefore, make sure that the rules of your hackathon already clearly define the later handling of the rights. You should seek legal assistance in this regard. Publish the rules in advance and make it clear in the registration form that by participating in the hackathon, participants fully accept the given rules. This way you are on the safe side and the participants are free to decide whether they want to participate or not under the given conditions, based on the handling of the rights you specify.

6.2   Criticism of Corporate Hackathons

As already described in Sect. 1.2, hackathons can have different goals. Internal company hackathons can be used as team building or recruiting events. Sometimes, however, hackathons are also interpreted as tough innovation machines that are supposed to ensure the success of a company under tremendous pressure. In the following the main points of criticism of internal hackathons are described.

- *Working time:* Since hackathons as described usually last a whole weekend, it is clear that overtime is indicated here. At best, the overtime will be compensated or paid. But there are also cases where participation in a hackathon is expected and the overtime is not counted. Here, the sociologist Sharon Zukin, who has studied hackathons extensively, speaks in plain language. She says that hackathons redefine precarious work as a great opportunity. Some companies, for example, use hackathons and their good reputation specifically to persuade employees to work unpaid overtime under great pressure to succeed (see [12]).

  Make sure in your company hackathons that participation is voluntary. Ordered overtime must be compensated or remunerated accordingly. This is clearly regulated. Of course, different rules apply to voluntary hackathons, which are intended to serve team building and not necessarily to pay into the company's innovation account.
- *Utilization:* It has already been criticized that hackathons are partly used to generate innovation under high pressure. But innovation and creativity cannot be forced. The company must be prepared for the fact that a hackathon potentially does not generate exploitable ideas. However, if a new business or product idea is generated, it is often not really converted into a real business. On the one hand, this demotivates the participants and, on the other hand, ensures that no further hackathons are held in the future because they have not shown any visible success.

  In order to avoid this trap, you should think about a process to further exploit the results of the hackathon already during the planning stage. Additionally, clarify who is responsible for this and how new ideas can be incorporated into your company. If this is not done, the ideas are often simply lost. So the hackathon has been in vain.

  It turns out that radical ideas in particular can overwhelm a company. But hackathons are supposed to encourage you to think completely different and to try out completely new approaches. Give the good ideas the chance to prove themselves. That way you can use the full potential of the hackathons.
- *Rights:* The subject of law has also already been dealt with. In contrast to open hackathons, criticism of in-house hackathons is not appropriate, since everything developed in an employee relationship for his employer belongs to the company. So the rules here are clear from the beginning. Nevertheless, if in doubt, you should communicate this again so that there are no problems.

- *Motivation:* Often it is also criticized that companies carry out hackathons out of the wrong motivation. The goal is then to present themselves to the outside world as a "hip and innovative" company. The actual event or even the possible result is then of secondary importance. This leads very quickly to demotivated employees because the actual purpose of the hackathons has been lost.

  If a hackathon is to be held as a team building activity, this should be clearly communicated. In addition, the expectations of the hackathon result should be adjusted accordingly. What counts here is not the best possible business idea, but the "we-feeling" of the participants during and after the hackathon. Please note that the energy from a hackathon usually dissipates after about 24 h and all participants have returned to their daily routine. So do not expect too much from such an event.

- *Employment:* Hackathons are often used as a recruiting event lately. Potential new employees should be observed during the event and their creativity, assertiveness, teamwork, and programming skills should be evaluated. Often the vacant positions are awarded as a prize for the best team. This puts a strain on the participants and turns a job interview into a competition that puts a lot of stress on all participants.

  If you are planning such hackathons, take the chance to get to know all participants and actively search for the best participants to fill your vacancies. Do not advertise the vacancies as a prize, but give everyone a fair chance to prove themselves. This will stress out the situation for everyone. In any case, you should conduct a classic job interview afterwards, as you have only experienced the participant in an extreme situation. In this case, you will have additional impressions after the interview which you can use for your personnel decision.

In all hackathons it should be noted that the participants take part voluntarily. Give the participants the opportunity to familiarize themselves with the rules, the operation, the handling of the rights, the evaluation criteria, and other circumstances in advance. So every participant can decide for himself if he wants to participate and how much effort he is willing to give. Accept the respective decision and use any criticism as a suggestion for optimization. If you keep this in mind, nothing should stand in the way of a successful hackathon.

6.3 Summary

- Apart from the good reputation of hackathons, the format is also only beginning to attract increasing criticism.
- Actively deal with the points of criticism and try to soften the points in your hackathons or avoid them completely by thorough planning.
- If possible, regulate all eventualities in advance and communicate all rules openly.

- Clarify in advance exactly what you expect from the hackathon and do not expect too much, as the results are not predictable.
- Please note that all participants take part voluntarily and respect the opinions and wishes of the participants.

Summary

7

Abstract

In this book a holistic overview of the current topic of hackathons was given. First of all the history of hackathons was explained. Afterwards the different goals of a hackathon were described. Subsequently, the three phases of hackathons, preparation, operation, and follow-up, were examined in detail with all aspects. Furthermore, not only the perspective of the organizer was taken, but also the participants' perspective was taken in a separate chapter and it was described what reasons for participation can be, how participants prepare themselves optimally and are as successful as possible. Finally, the criticism of the format was given space and solutions were offered.

In this book a holistic overview about hackathons was given. More and more popular events were illuminated from different perspectives. Therefore this book is not only for organizers of hackathons (no matter if public or company hackathons), but also for participants or people generally interested in this topic.

At first the history and the development of the hackathons were shown. The events coming from the USA have developed in the last years from small (mostly privately organized events) to big events with more than thousand participants and corresponding media support. In the beginning, the first hackathons were attended by technology enthusiasts who wanted to try out new technology in small local groups, fix their problems, and push them to their limits. Nowadays, this has developed into a wide variety of formats with the most diverse goals worldwide. Hackathons have become highly commercialized in recent years and have become the motor of an entire start-up generation. In hackathons new business ideas are tested and presented to potential investors. Often new companies are founded or ideas are bought by large corporations directly after hackathons. Hackathons are not only held in public. Companies also appreciate the modern and agile format to quickly develop innovative ideas within the company.

© The Author(s), under exclusive license to Springer Nature Switzerland AG 2020   83
A. Kohne, V. Wehmeier, *Hackathons*,
https://doi.org/10.1007/978-3-030-58839-7_7

Hackathons can be divided into three phases. The first phase includes the preparation of the actual event. Here the foundation for a successful event is laid. Among other things, it is necessary to define exactly who the organizer is, which participants the event is aimed at and with what goal, where and with what equipment and technology the event will be held, what the organizer team looks like, and which legal aspects have to be considered. In the second phase the hackathon will be held. Here again three major partial aspects can be defined. At the beginning of a hackathon is the start phase, in which the actual event is introduced. The motto, the technologies used, the procedure, and further rules are presented. Often a thematically fitting impulse lecture is given here. Afterwards the participants present their possible topics and ideas and the teams are formed according to their interests. Then the actual work phase begins, in which the participants work out their ideas. In the final phase, the participants present their work results to a jury and the other participants. The best results are then awarded prizes. After that the hackathon is officially over. But now the third and often forgotten phase of the follow-up work begins. First of all an evaluation of the event is made from the feedback of the participants and the team and possible improvements for the next event are recorded as "lessons learned." Furthermore, all participants and the sponsors should be thanked and a follow-up report should be made online and in the classic media. Additionally, the participants should be offered help in continuing their projects. An alumni network can be founded for this purpose or experts can be sent to help. Finally, the sustainability of the elaborated results should be ensured in a suitable form. This will ensure that the hackathon was a complete success for everyone.

Furthermore, the book also takes the participants' view. Different reasons for participating in a hackathon were presented. Furthermore, tips were given, which should help to participate in a hackathon as successfully as possible. Furthermore, it was described how participants prepare themselves optimally for a hackathon and what they can do after an event to really take advantage of all the benefits of the format.

Finally, the criticism of hackathons was presented. Especially the criticism of commercialization and thus the reversal of the original idea of hackathons were described. Furthermore, topics like the lack of sleep, nutrition, and the potential exploitation of the participants were described and possible solutions were offered.

We hope that you enjoyed the book and that it gave you a well-founded, comprehensive, and multi-faceted insight into the popular event format of hackathons. For your next hackathon, whether as organizer or participant, we wish you success.

Outlook

8

Abstract

Hackathons have become established all over the world in recent years. At present, a movement back to the roots of the events can be observed. Away from the huge commercially oriented events to small rounds that turn again to trying out and expanding technology. In addition, hackathons will also conquer other industries as digitalization progresses. So the future hackathons will continue to develop, but the format as such will continue to exist.

Much has been written in this book about the history and present of hackathons. But it is also worthwhile to take a look into the future because hackathons will continue to be a very important event format.

After the focus of many hackathons in the last years was put on the mediation of investor money and mainly commercial goals were pursued, the calls for hackathons in their original form became louder recently. Hackathons have changed from small meetings in the basement of an acquaintance to fully organized mega meetings with sponsors and huge prize money. These kinds of events are getting more and more into disrepute, especially with the true "hackers" and "makers," as they often go against their own values and convictions. It can be observed that in many places groups of technology enthusiasts are again joining forces to try out new technology, push it to its limits, and supplement it in a meaningful way. This was exactly the idea of the first hackathons. Thus a movement back to the roots can be observed, which will certainly continue and above all fits into the zeitgeist of the maker scene, which has made it its goal to find quick, simple, and self-developed solutions to everyday problems. This scene is again more to be assigned to the open source scene, which does not pursue any commercial goals and rather focuses on free exchange of opinions and information. The pure fun of trying things out is once again the focus of attention. The pressure to be spontaneously innovative under time constraints and the critical eyes of sponsors, investors, and the jury is thus eliminated. This creates space for completely new and creative ideas.

Surely there will still be commercially oriented hackathons. The interest of investors and sponsors is much too great for that. In addition, the ever-growing shortage of skilled workers, especially in IT, will ensure that modern recruiting formats such as hackathons will become the norm rather than sensational individual events.

Furthermore, IT and digital technology will enter many additional areas over the next few years as digitalization continues to advance. Thus, in the future there will be hackathons in areas that have not been in the foreground so far. For example, in the medical and pharmaceutical industries, hackathons are already being increasingly performed. This will certainly increase in the future and additional industries will want to take advantage of the benefits of hackathons.

Hackathons will therefore continue to accompany us and will continue to bring people together to try out technology, solve problems, learn together, exchange ideas with like-minded people and perhaps make the world a better place.

Quotations

9

Abstract

In this chapter we have collected voices from industry and administration on the subject of hackathons. Each of the different statements is given as a quotation.

We have made very good experiences with Hackathons. Especially the result orientation and the community approach behind hackathons have a great impact. - Result orientation. Developers can train their working technique with Hackathons. They have to organize themselves in a way that at the end there is a result. - Community: In a community action really thick boards can be drilled and creative solutions can be invented. The community does not have to be limited to one company. It gets really cool in a hackathon when people with different talents from different companies work together to create something.

Dr. Josef Adersberger, CTO, QAware GmbH

—

Hackathons offer an excellent platform for small teams with clear time and location specifications to tackle dedicated questions and problem solutions in a goal-oriented manner - and undisturbed by daily tasks. The implicit competitive character contributes to a very positive and constructive working atmosphere. The concluding presentations, which are limited in time for all teams, summarize the two to three day events in a very impressive and entertaining way.

Harry K. Baur—Manager, Business Operations Data and AI, IBM Germany Research and Development, Böblingen

—

The BMVI Data Run, which took place on 22 and 23 March 2019 in Berlin, was the fourth hackathon organised by the Federal Ministry of Transport and Digital Infrastructure (BMVI). The goal of the BMVI Data Run is to generate new innovative ideas within about 24 hours based on data from the BMVI's business area that have been collected by public authorities or scientific institutions for a completely different purpose. The added value is created by combining data from different sources and using them in new digital applications. This requires a good portion of creativity, innovative strength and passion of the participants! The passion of some teams even reached so far in past hackathons that they developed a project out of their idea that originated at the BMVI Data Run. This project was subsequently funded by the research initiative mFUND of the BMVI. This shows us that the Hackathon format is not only a unique 24-hour event, but the ideas and solutions developed have potential for data-based research projects for Mobility 4.0. The BMVI not only has a great interest in data innovations, but is also the department with the most data-bearing authorities. That is why we feel particularly committed to the Open Data principle.

Steffen Bilger, Parliamentary State Secretary at the German Federal Ministry of Transport and Digital Infrastructure

—

Hackathons are an excellent opportunity for students to demonstrate not only their technical skills but also their ability to work in a team in a competition. Solving difficult problems with great commitment in a limited time creates motivation and enthusiasm. Of course, the prizes awarded must also be appropriate.

Hans Decker, Chairman of the Board of Alumi Informatik at the TU Dortmund University, Germany

—

Hackathons are an excellent opportunity at Leibniz Universität Hannover and the Faculty of Electrical Engineering and Computer Science to offer students an attractive range of courses with a high practical relevance outside of their everyday studies. From the point of view of the faculty and lecturers, there are several advantages here. For example, students can be given tasks with a high research or industrial reference that can arouse their interest in a specific topic. Participating companies have the opportunity to present themselves as attractive employers and to introduce their own topics. In the course of the hackathon, the students generally get to know new technologies and frameworks and thus expand their specialist knowledge. Furthermore, they deepen their ability to organize, work on and present projects in groups under time pressure. Last but not least, the teachers can get in touch with the students outside the usual study situation and get to know each other better. For the reasons mentioned above, the Faculty of Electrical Engineering and Computer Science organizes hackathons with various partners, e.g. Microsoft, regional companies, or the university's start-up service, time and again.

Prof. Dr. Ralph Ewerth, Prof. Dr. Michael Rohs, Leibniz University of Hannover, Germany

—

Hackathons offer companies an excellent opportunity to investigate a new technology for technical feasibility and potential challenges within a very short time. Crucial for success is an interdisciplinary, personally and culturally diverse background of the participants, which combines different perspectives.

Uwe Gruenefeld, Senior Researcher, OFFIS - Institute for Information Technology, University of Oldenburg, Germany

—

For us at SUSE, the hackathons that we have been holding around the world since 2007 under the name "SUSE Hack Week" play a very important role for employees and businesses alike.

This week without pressure and set goals is used by the SUSE technology community for creative thinking and the implementation of ideas for various open source projects as well as their own favorite projects. About 650 like-minded developers work together in this global hackathon, which has a nerdy character, and all professional technical company resources are available. Each SUSE Hack Week includes a dedicated program of events, including food and beverage, events, and of course SUSE-sponsored clothing and iconic gifts. Genuine crowd working, with a minimum of rules, which works extremely well with the soon to be 18th SUSE Hack Week.

SUSE Hack Week is also a huge success for the company. On the one hand, it acts as an incubator for innovations, some of which can later be incorporated into products as new features. On the other hand, despite the large number of participants at different locations around the world, our Hackathon creates a creative workshop atmosphere. There is plenty of time for exchange and getting to know each other, for example through project teams from different areas or meet & greet opportunities at breakfast and lunches. This hub approach ensures that silos and barriers of thought do not arise within the large, globally distributed SUSE developer community. Many of our partners also take advantage of the opportunity to participate in SUSE Hack Week. A hackathon is like a giant "sandbox" in which to pursue entirely new approaches in areas such as artificial intelligence or the Internet of Things. For an innovative company like SUSE, encouraging our employees to be creative and think outside the box is an integral part of our corporate culture.

Roland Haidl, Director Operations and Services, SUSE

—

Hackathons are a brilliant format to try out new ideas - and a great experience for the participants.

Uwe Hansmann—Senior Leader Watson Customer Engagement Development, IBM Germany Research and Development, Böblingen

—

For the Federal Office of Administration, the central service authority of the Federal Government, digital issues are part of its core business. Ambitious IT experts and young professionals can find a wealth of exciting topics and projects here: The digitalization of the asylum procedure, passenger data storage, electronic processing of visa applications - we handle these and other tasks on behalf of various federal ministries. But it is not only in terms of content that we are one of the most versatile employers. More than many private companies, we can also respond to the personal needs of our employees: family-friendly flexible working hours and mobile working play a major role at the BVA.

But: How many of the well-trained specialists we are looking for already know this? Which IT-oriented career starter thinks of public administration when planning for the future? And how does the BVA get itself into contact with young people?

With Hackathons - as we know since our first attempt with this format!

Together with Microsoft Germany, Bundesdruckerei and Governikus KG, the BVA 2017 organised a hackathon for modernising administration. More than 40 students, trainees, IT specialists from the public sector and other IT enthusiasts took part in the two-day event in Berlin. For 24 hours they were supposed to think about the future, develop creative ideas and approaches to solutions. The hope to inspire creative people from the IT and technology sectors to join the BVA with this event was fulfilled. The participants recognized: Interdisciplinary teams, communication at eye level, solution-oriented project work on concrete problems, an early testing of ideas, the "getting on the road" of new concepts - the Hackathon principle and the BVA fit together perfectly. And: To realize exciting IT ideas and at the same time keep the work-life balance, public administration is a place with many opportunities.

Sabine Lang, Head of the Strategic Control Unit, Federal Office of Administration, Germany

—

Hackathons are for me a proven means to create a free space in a working day dominated by IT routine, where creativity can be given free rein and unfinished ideas can be pursued. In other words, a space is created where you can spin to your heart's content. The strong focus on time automatically ensures that prototypes are created that convey a core idea instead of aiming for completeness. In addition, getting to know new people and the casual networking that ensues allows you to look beyond your own nose. Experience has shown that this view expands one's own knowledge and understanding on the one hand and on the other hand very often leads to new ideas. If you take the HR perspective from the employer's point of view, then Hackathons are a very valuable building block for us in employee retention as well as in employer branding. However, they must not be an alibi event, but must be established with the necessary seriousness and their results followed up. And by the way, Hackathons are also a lot of fun.

Dr. André Marburger, Head of Development, REWE Systems GmbH, Germany

—

In a time of constant need for innovation, hackathons offer a perfect playground for every player in society. Companies can experience start-up business models as solutions are created in smaller teams. Universities get an insight into the latest challenges and solutions. However, it is the students who benefit the most: they exercise innovation and creativity in a short period of time.

Olha Mikhieieva, Project Manager, CGI

—

Jörn Ossowski and Annett Nagel - the two initiators of the thyssenkrupp Hackathon #hack4tk - are currently preparing the fourth Hackathon (July 2019). "We are pleased that the series has established itself. It shows how innovative and open thyssenkrupp is as a Group for new ideas and methods," says Annett Nagel. Above all, thyssenkrupp expects one thing from the Hackathon itself: plenty of new digital approaches for the future of the company and much faster testing of the approaches. "At the hackathon, our participants generate fresh ideas because, as outsiders, they bring different perspectives and skills with them," explains Jörn Ossowski. He continues: "This way, prototypes are developed for real business challenges within 24 hours. The best ones are subsequently brought to product maturity with the teams".

Dr. Annett Nagel, Head of Agile/DT & Change, Group Processes & Information Technology, thyssenkrupp

—

In many large companies such as Microsoft, Facebook & Co. the Hackathon culture has long since contributed to the creation of corporate value, not in the sense of a technical programming exercise, but always with regard to a concrete customer problem. The focus of a hackathon is on innovative problem solving: it is about working together on a complex problem and developing a practical and workable solution for a given problem or task within a certain short period of time. This interdisciplinary approach ensures that (product) solutions of companies are analysed at an early stage with all their consequences and possible dead ends are avoided.

Dr. Kim Nguyen, cryptologist and head of Trusted Services at Bundesdruckerei GmbH, Germany

—

The nice thing about the Blockchain-Hackathons I have experienced so far was the noticeable positive spirit in the air. Starting with the formation of the teams up to the absolute highlight: the presentation.

The great thing about a hackathon is that individuals grow together very quickly and work together as a team. People who often didn't know each other before, find intuitive solutions together within days or even hours. Completely detached from fixed structures and "old habits". At the end of a hackathon it often does not matter who the "winner" is. All teams together contribute to the success of the hackathon.

I also find the organization of hackathons extremely exciting for companies. Where else do you get such access to talent and know-how and at the same time strengthen your employer branding.

Mark Preus, CEO BTC-ECHO GmbH, Kleve, Germany

—

Hackathons have now established themselves as a proven and promising format for recruiting new employees, for the "quick" creation of new (business) ideas and for low-threshold testing of possible potentials of technological innovations. A further added value, which is often neglected in the overall assessment, is the smart testing of new alliances that are created around the execution of a hackathon. This is because it often successfully brings together players from different fields of activity and even sectors and their respective potentials, who would either not have come together at all or only at significantly higher costs without a hackathon.

Johannes Rosenboom, Vice President Public Sector, Sales Marketing Business Development, Materna Information & Communications SE, Dortmund, Germany

—

The Hackathon does not only have an external effect, with which the organizer wants to attract applicants or innovative ideas for selected tasks. The Hackathon always has an internal effect on the organizer's organization, which should also be taken into account when planning the event. What effect can the new ideas have in my organization? Which inspiration can be derived for my own innovation processes? How can I win over my own teams to participate in the Hackathons? With your own teams, the Hackathon can also be used specifically to promote your own young talents and your own innovative ability.

Alexander Schmid, Partner, BearingPoint

—

I am a big fan of hackathons when it comes to trying a new idea and getting results fast. Especially important to me is the aspect of working solution-oriented in a cross-functional group on an innovation or something new, without departmental battles or company policy unnecessarily slowing down. The result must then speak for itself. Decisions about value contribution and the usefulness of innovations can usually be assessed much better after the hackathon.

Denny Schreber, Senior Solution Architect, cbs Corporate Business Solutions Management Consulting GmbH, Germany

—

In Hackathons (and all other crowdsourcing competitions) communication is the key to success. This applies to the organizer as well as the participants. Questions need to be answered about who, when, which and how information is shared. Perhaps the most important aspect of communication in Hackathons is the feedback of the organizer for the participants. Only if participants learn why their solution was (not) chosen, they can learn from it and consider the competition a success. Without this feedback, the motivation to participate in a hackathon again in the future dwindles, frustration about the perceived waste of time spreads and the fear of the organizer to have worked out a solution for nothing in return is omnipresent. Therefore it is important for hackathon organizers to design the communication strategy in advance and to share it with the participants.

Dr. Sebastian Schäfer, Head of Innovation, Schmiede Zollverein GmbH, Essen, Germany

—

Hackathons have become more than just pizza and late nights. Instead, they offer an opportunity to test new ideas in a playful and unbureaucratic way, to build prototypes and to concretize cost estimates. At the same time, hackathons are the best way to familiarize yourself with new technologies in a practical way in the fast-moving cloud age.

Clemens Siebler, Cloud Solution Architect, Microsoft Deutschland GmbH

—

Hackathons provide an excellent setting for an event with a positive competitive character and a spirit of optimism among like-minded people. Therefore, they typically produce far more innovation and "disruption" than the actual task might initially seem.

Sven Stueven—Executive Assistant, IBM Germany Research and Development

—

Hackathons have a unique flair. You work together, desperately, cheer and try to make the world a little better with a few ideas. Even if many of the projects don't find their way into our everyday lives, there is always a little spark of inspiration at the end.

Heike Zöller, Online Marketing Manager, Business Academy Ruhr, Dortmund, Germany

Checklists

10

Abstract

Hackathons are complex events. They require elaborate and careful planning. In this chapter you will find checklists that can serve as a reminder or template. This way you will not forget anything important during all activities around your next hackathon (no matter if you are the organizer or a participant) and you can concentrate on the concrete elaboration.

A hackathon is a special format among the event types. While many forms of events welcome and inform the participants and bid them farewell without obligation, the hackathon is different. On the part of the participants and the organizer it has to be considered how to use the planned common time optimally, how to have it comfortable over a longer period of time and above all: What you get from this event at the end and what commonalities arise. The special nature of this format makes it predestined to forget or not properly consider things due to the complexity of the various tasks. Simple checklists are helpful here to collect one's own thoughts and start a hackathon in a structured way.

In the following you will find checklists which you can use as a reminder or copy template when planning your hackathon activities.

10.1   Lists for Preparation

Below is a list of possible communication media you can use to promote your hackathon, as well as a list of activities you should consider when planning your hackathon:

10.1.1 Media for Communication

- The own internet presence should promote the hackathon event in the category "events." Also all information about the event as well as the registration link should be found here.
- Viral marketing via acquaintances, social media and co. should be started early. An info e-mail can also be circulated to forward to friends and acquaintances. Social media channels can be used in advance for advertising, as well as for later live reporting.
- Paper is not always "old-school"—on a university campus or on a company notice board you should also use a small poster or flyer.
- A media partnership involves greater planning effort and also costs, but allows for target-group-specific approaches to potential participants.
- The name and the motto of the event have a great influence on the perception of potential participants and thus also on the interest in participating. The name of the event should be indicative of the topic and also show what kind of event it is.
- The possible advertising measures may (in the spirit of a hackathon) be allowed to be unusual.

10.1.2 Activities in Preparation

Activities Before the Hackathon

- In the first phases of the hackathon preparation you should already think about the target audience and possible participants. A mixed audience is an advantage and as long as equal opportunities are maintained, the best ingredient for a successful hackathon.
- The duration of the planned hackathon is decisive for the expected preparation effort but also the expected results. Challenging topics require more time. Simple hackathon topics can also be implemented in shorter periods of time with less preparation in terms of infrastructure and support.
- The legal aspects of a hackathon should be kept in mind, but they should not spoil the fun of the hackathon. Rules of the game and all agreements should be known very early on and should be recorded in writing. The exploitation rights require special attention.
- The right venue is also attractive for the participants, but must also be suitable for a hackathon. Accessibility, attractiveness, and spaciousness are possible aspects of the choice of location.
- The equipment and technology in the hackathon requires a lot of attention, but is critical to the success of almost any hackathon project these days. Not everything has to be bought. Also renting, lending, or Bring-Your-Own-Device (BYOD) are possible solutions. A check for completeness and function must be done before the hackathon event.

- The organizing team must be clearly defined, sufficiently dimensioned, and coordinated in its roles.
- Volunteers from the organization or from partners should be informed early on about the special challenge of a hackathon so that they too can prepare themselves sufficiently.
- The costs of a hackathon can be planned, but a buffer for all cases is advisable.
- Much can be done by yourself, support from agencies is professional, but increases the budget requirements.
- The financing and the choice of sponsors must be thought through in the first round of the hackathon planning. This is where the overall budget and the proportional distribution of costs are decided, as well as the right of co-determination of the individual participants.
- The prizes to be awarded should not be the main focus of the participants, but should also be a real incentive especially for young people. Non-cash prizes have an advertising effect and can also be given out in larger numbers as smaller prizes, depending on their type and value.
- The composition and work of the jury must be transparent and comprehensible. The evaluation criteria must be formulated very clearly in advance.

10.2 Lists for Operation

The implementation of the hackathon event is divided into the start phase, the work phase, and the final phase. Organizer and participants have different shares in the process during these phases. In the following you will find a list of all points that are important for the operation of your hackathon:

10.2.1 Activities in Operation

Activities at the Hackathon

- Before the participants arrive, name badges should be printed out and organizational issues clarified. General questions of the participants or questions about the organization should not come up so often during the actual execution of the event.
- It should be clear to each participant beforehand what to expect at the hackathon. This includes the questions of personal preparation, the expected participation in the hackathon, but also the burden that awaits him.
- The pre-program of a hackathon should inform and motivate. It should not be long-winded and should convey appreciation for the participants through selected top-class speakers.

- Organizational matters, rules, and procedures should be explained several times, especially if these points are of central importance. This should be done one last time before the actual start of the work phase.
- Pointing out the possibilities for generating ideas should be considered an offer, but not an obligation. Coaching the teams is useful, but should not distort competition.
- The question possibilities for participants before the actual start should be scheduled. Most of the questions should be clarified in advance through signage or handouts.
- The distribution of roles in the teams should be clarified. The organizer is allowed to point out a reasonable division in advance.
- The prizes to be won should be presented. It is even more important to make the valuation rules for obtaining the prizes transparent.
- The motto and the goals of the hackathon are to be explained in detail. Every participant must know for himself that he is working on the right task.
- The beginning of the hackathon should be made exciting with panels, keynotes, or other motivating points.
- The work phase may not only be observed, but may also be proactively accompanied by the organizer. Attention must be paid to compliance with the fairness rules as well as to possible overstraining of teams.
- The evaluation sheets (how did you like the hackathon) are important for the follow-up and should be brought to the audience without disturbance in the second half of the work phase. The wish to collect the completed evaluation forms must be repeated several times.
- The preparation of the presentation is up to the participants, but may be coached by the organizer. Here the time management is very important.
- The type of presentation should either be precisely defined or completely left up to the teams. The presentation mix of the participants has to be implemented by the organizer.
- Throughout the entire event, time must be kept in mind; announcements about the remaining working time should be made regularly and discreetly.
- The last hour of the work phase should be used for final checks, but also to prepare the participants for an end of the active phase.

10.3 Lists for Follow-Up

Below is a list of possible success metrics for measuring your hackathon, as well as a list of all activities that are important in the follow-up to your event:

10.3.1 Success Metrics

Success Metrics

- The evaluation of the forms reflects the mood of the participants. The evaluation, e.g. by means of school grades on organization, invitation procedure, design, catering, etc., makes it easier to look back.
- The mood of the participants and their comments after the event give an impression of whether the course and end of the event were assessed as good and fair by the participants. This subjective impression should not be underestimated and is the sum of the impressions of the organizers and partners.
- The partners' assessment of the event gives an impression of whether their expectations were met. A separate evaluation sheet can be used here.
- At the end of the competition, the results of the jury can provide an indication of the quality and practical applicability of the team's performance. For example, a well-thought-out idea already provided with a realistic market entry strategy can be considered a success.
- Concrete reactions such as spontaneous offers of cooperation or venture capital show how sustainable results are assessed.
- The post-event reporting and the reactions in social media provide information on how the course of the hackathon and the results are assessed from outside.
- After and during the event, the number of reports, the "likes" and "shares," and the reach of the reports on the social platforms can be measured.
- The interest of the participants and partners to keep in touch afterwards can be seen as positive.
- Due to partnerships, start-ups, and the follow-up of ideas, the evaluation of sustainable results can only take place weeks or months later. These results may also be communicated to all participants and partners.

10.3.2 Activities in Follow-Up

Activities After the Hackathon

- The review and assessment of what one has done well and what one can do better in the future should be a duty in the follow-up. To this end, carry out an open and honest "lessons learned" and use the results for continuous improvement.
- Say thank you to all participants and the contributors on the organizer side! This is more than appropriate in view of the efforts made and helps to motivate participation in further events.
- The post-award reporting should not stop after the award ceremony, but should be carried out in detail in the post-award follow-up. Even after a few weeks, reporting on possible sustainable results is still useful.

- Under no circumstances should the processing of the results be postponed. The impression of a hackathon must be freshly incorporated into the follow-up.
- Support should be provided to participants who want to develop their results further. This should be done in a purely pragmatic way by continuing the coaching, if necessary also in a concrete cooperation based on partnership. The organizer should also support cooperation among participants or partners that arise from the event (even if the organizer does not benefit directly).
- Possible job interviews or discussions about job offers should be taken up directly afterwards. Just a few days between hackathon and renewed contact can cool down the mutual enthusiasm between potential employer and applicant. Therefore there is no time to lose here.
- An alumni network for the hackathon event should be initiated as a social media thread. This requires at least some attention during the subsequent maintenance and moderation.
- Ideas on sustainability and future hackathon events should be recorded and followed up. Written form is mandatory here, so that essential ideas are not forgotten.

10.4   Lists for Participants

In the following you will find lists for possible participants of a hackathon.

10.4.1 Reasons for Participation

Reasons for Participation

- Do I want to go well beyond my limits? Do I have fun testing myself?
- Do I want to develop an idea beyond the end of the hackathon?
- Is there any interest in embarking on a greater adventure, e.g. by realizing a new idea born in the hackathon?
- Do I enjoy doing unconventional things?
- Is there a chance to make a small idea bigger with others?
- Am I maybe a potential start-up entrepreneur?
- Am I interested in becoming part of expert networks?
- Do I want to prove myself as a potential employee with an employer?

10.4.2 Personal Preparation

Personal Preparation

- Dealing with the motto of the hackathon and building up initial sketches of ideas helps to quickly gain momentum later.
- The organizer's organizational instructions must be studied carefully. The rules of the game may decide whether to participate or not.
- The rules of the organizer determine to what extent one is willing to submit ideas on behalf of the organizer. Do I want to do that?
- I must inform my personal environment that I will not be available for a longer period of time.
- A good rest before the event is advantageous for a continuous waking phase over a long period of time.
- Good basic technical equipment is mandatory.
- A collection of the preferred development tools should be pre-installed.
- Prepared slide templates can greatly facilitate the creation of the presentation.
- It does not always have to be the goal of winning first place. A hackathon has much more to offer.

10.4.3 Packing List for Participants

Packing List for Participants (See Chap. 2)

- Laptop with appropriate software (development tools, presentation tools, image editing software, etc.)
- Laptop and mobile phone charger (optional: power bank)
- Keyboard and mouse (optional)
- USB stick and/or external hard disk
- Pencil and paper
- Backpack and small carrying bag (for promotional gifts, prices, and brochures)
- Deodorant
- Toothbrush and toothpaste
- Additional change of clothes (pyjamas if desired)
- Towel
- Soap and/or shower gel
- Antibacterial wipes and/or disinfection spray
- Sleeping bag, blanket, and pillow
- Refillable bottle
- Possibly needed medicine
- Earplugs
- Possibly special hardware and tools for hardware hacks

- If desired: music (on mobile phone or other device) and headphones (with noise reduction if possible)
- Optional: books and (card) games for breaks

10.4.4 Personal Follow-Up

Personal Follow-Up

- Was the hackathon motto realistic?
- Were the conditions fair and predictable?
- Were the teams sufficiently supported and did the organizer keep promises?
- Do the announcements and the course of the event coincide with the implementation?
- Were there enough clues for a good preparation and was I well informed?
- Were the conditions for a hackathon appropriate?
- Did I have fun at the event?
- Do I have sustainable advantages through new ideas, new acquaintances, or a new job?
- Do I want to keep in touch with new acquaintances? If so, in what way?

10.5   Templates for Feedback Forms

In the following you will find lists of possible questionnaires which you can make available to your participants, sponsors and exhibitors, investors, and your team after your hackathon in order to receive extensive feedback. Please note that many questions from the participant feedback can also be used in the other questionnaires. Therefore, the other lists only contain additional questions.

10.5.1 Participant Feedback

Questions to Participants

- How satisfied were you overall with the hackathon?
- How satisfied were you with the preparation?
- Were the premises suitable?
- Were you satisfied with the catering?
- Were they satisfied with the time available?
- Was the communication in advance sufficient?
- Did you always have a contact person and enough support?

- What did you think of the choice of topics?
- Were you satisfied with the social program?
- Did you have time for (professional) exchange during the event?
- Was the award ceremony fair?
- Did you see the prizes as an incentive to participate?
- In your opinion, was the result of the jury evaluation transparent?
- What sustainable benefit could you gain from the event?
- How can we improve the preparation/operation/follow-up for the next time?
- Would you be interested in a next hackathon?
- Do you have any other comments?

10.5.2 Sponsor Feedback

Questions to Sponsors

- At which points were your expectations fulfilled/not fulfilled?
- Did you feel adequately represented as a sponsor?
- Are you satisfied with the feedback of the participants?
- Will the event be considered a success, economically or ideally?
- Have you made any new interesting contacts?
- Can you rate the event on a scale of 1–10 regarding to your expectations?
- What can you/we do better on a rerun?

10.5.3 Investor Feedback

Questions for Investors

- Can you use the results of the hackathon for your own progress?
- Have you been presented with interesting ideas/concepts/business models?
- Will you subsequently invest in a (newly founded) company?
- Was the effort in proportion to the success?
- Would you like to help shape such a format one more time?
- What would you do differently next time?

10.5.4 Team Feedback

Questions for the Team

- Was the stress reasonable?

- Does the planning match the result?
- Was there something that stood out particularly positively/negatively during the event?
- Were you sufficiently prepared?
- Would you participate in another hackathon?
- Was the hackathon a meaningful event for you (or the company)?
- Which processes worked as planned and which did not?
- Where was the trouble?
- Where did the participants have the most problems/questions?
- Was there something missing that you should definitely think about next time?
- What were the highlights (positive and negative)?

References

1. T. Boden. The grid enterprise - structuring the agile business of the future. *BT technology journal*, 22(1):107–117, 2004.
2. John Cheesman and John Daniels. *UML components*. Addison-Wesley Reading, 2001.
3. Jonathan Gottfried. A brief history of hackathons. https://www.youtube.com/watch?v=Zr6VPAe9CKU, March 2014.
4. Jonathan Gottfried. History of Hackathons - Revised for HackCon. https://de.slideshare.net/JonMarkGo/history-of-hackathons-revised-for-hackcon, February 2014.
5. Mark Hatch. *The maker movement manifesto: Rules for innovation in the new world of crafters, hackers, and tinkerers*. McGraw-Hill Education New York, 2014.
6. Jessica Keyes. *Bring your own devices (BYOD) survival guide*. CRC press, 2013.
7. Andreas Kohne. *Business Development: Customer-oriented Business Development for Successful Companies*. Springer, 2019.
8. Jeanne Liedtka and Tim Ogilvie. *Designing for growth: A design thinking tool kit for managers*. Columbia University Press, 2011.
9. Alexander Osterwalder and Yves Pigneur. *Business model generation: a handbook for visionaries, game changers, and challengers*. John Wiley & Sons, 2010.
10. Kenneth S Rubin. *Essential Scrum: A practical guide to the most popular Agile process*. Addison-Wesley, 2012.
11. Shalini Verma. *Enhancing employability soft skills*. Pearson Education India, 2012.
12. Sharon Zukin and Max Papadantonakis. Hackathons as co-optation ritual: Socializing workers and institutionalizing innovation in the "new" economy. In *Precarious work*. Emerald Publishing Limited, 2017.

© The Author(s), under exclusive license to Springer Nature Switzerland AG 2020
A. Kohne, V. Wehmeier, *Hackathons*,
https://doi.org/10.1007/978-3-030-58839-7

Index

The manufacturer's authorised representative in the EU is Springer
Nature Customer Service Centre GmbH, Europaplatz 3, 69115 Heidelberg,
Germany. If you have any concerns regarding our products, please
contact ProductSafety@springernature.com

Printed and bound by CPI Group (UK) Ltd, Croydon, CR0 4YY
24/04/2026
02096340-0008